SUDAN

TITLES IN THE MODERN NATIONS OF THE WORLD SERIES INCLUDE:

Afghanistan	Jordan
Argentina	Kenya
Australia	Lebanon
Austria	Liberia
Bolivia	Mexico
Brazil	Nigeria
Cambodia	North Korea
Canada	Norway
China	Pakistan
Congo	Peru
Cuba	Philippines
Czech Republic	Poland
Egypt	Russia
England	Saudi Arabia
Ethiopia	Scotland
Finland	Somalia
France	South Africa
Germany	South Korea
Greece	Spain
Haiti	Sweden
Hungary	Switzerland
India	Taiwan
Iran	Thailand
Iraq	Turkey
Ireland	United States
Israel	Vietnam
Italy	Yemen
Japan	

MODERN
NATIONS
—OF THE—
WORLD

SUDAN

BY SALOME C. NNOROMELE

LUCENT
BOOKS ®

THOMSON
—✳—
™
GALE

San Diego • Detroit • New York • San Francisco • Cleveland • New Haven, Conn. • Waterville, Maine • London • Munich

THOMSON
GALE

LIBRARY OF CONGRESS CATALOGING-IN-PUBLICATION DATA

Nnoromele, Salome C., 1967–
  Sudan / by Salome Nnoromele.
    p. cm. — (Modern nations of the world)
Summary: Examines the land, people, and history of Sudan, and discusses its current
state of affairs and place in the world today, including the strife between black and
Arab Sudanese.
Includes bibliographical references and index.
  ISBN 1-59018-338-X
  1. Sudan—Juvenile literature. [1. Sudan.] I. Title. II. Series.
  DT154.6.N665 2004
  962.4—dc22
                                                                        2003012199

Printed in the United States of America

CONTENTS

INTRODUCTION

Two Nations

Bilad al Sudan, Arabic for Land of the Blacks, was the term used by Arab geographers to describe the land lying south of the Sahara desert in Africa. The present Democratic Republic of Sudan occupies part of this region and takes its name from the term. But modern Sudan is not a country of just black Africa. Because of its various contacts with Arab immigrants from the north, as well as immigrants from other parts of Africa, Sudan today is home to many ethnic groups with different languages, histories, religious practices, and ways of life. These ethnic groups fall into two larger racial categories —Arab Africans and black Africans. Arabs live in the central and northern parts of the country, and most of them practice varying forms of the Islamic faith. Black Africans claim the southern part of the country as their homeland; most practice the African traditional religion of belief in many gods (animism), and a few are Christian or Muslim.

The mixture of Arabs and black Africans, with varying religious beliefs and culture, in Sudan has not been peaceful. Historically Arabs and black Africans in Sudan have not perceived themselves as one people. Each claims a separate heritage and identity. Many scholars familiar with the complex history of Sudan see the country as a land consisting of two hostile nations—one belonging to the Arabs, the other to black Africans. In the past, northern Sudan, home to Sudanese Arabs, basically saw its neighbor to the south simply as a source for slaves to be exported to other countries, especially Egypt, for use as farm laborers, domestic servants, concubines, or military mercenaries. Southern peoples saw the northerners as threats to their survival and strove to protect themselves from slave raiding and other violations of their sovereignty. There was, then, very little friendly contact between the north and the south.

During the nineteenth century, the Egyptians and their British colonial overlords dominated Sudan and reinforced those traditional hostilities, believing that it was in the interest of the colonial enterprise to maintain the divisions between the two peoples. Consequently, northern and southern Sudan were governed as separate political and cultural entities.

The policy of separate administrations for the peoples of Sudan may have worked for the colonial regime, but in the years since the nation gained its independence on January 1, 1956, Sudanese have had difficulty seeing themselves as members of one nation with a common political goal. Since its independence the country has been embroiled in civil war for all but ten years. The civil war has its roots in the southerners' resentment against the northerners, who they

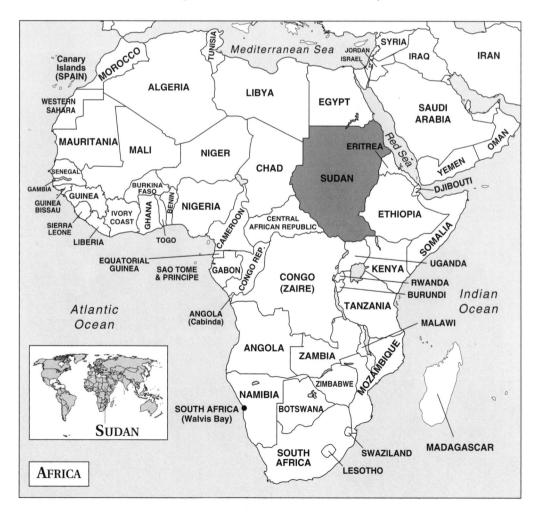

*Former prime minister
Isma'il al-Azhari
(center) is jubilant after
Sudan wins
independence from
Britain in January
1956. Since gaining
independence, Sudan
has been plagued by
civil war.*

feel are trying to dominate and marginalize them both politically and economically. The northerners, who for the most
part have ruled the country since independence, have intensified the southerners' fears by trying to impose Islam
and the Islamic way of life on the southerners, a majority of
whom are not Muslim.

The civil war has resulted in massive destruction, especially in the south, where most of the fighting takes place.
Many lives have been lost in what many observers consider
the most complex war on the African continent. Some
southern Sudanese have migrated to the north to avoid the
fighting; others have migrated to neighboring African countries and to nations elsewhere in the world, including the

United States, as refugees. By fleeing, these Sudanese find safety. "But their standard of living in these relocated places," as one Sudanese remarks, "is below what it would have been had the people been living in their own homelands."[1] Many of these refugees are poor and live in squalid conditions. In addition, as the people are exiled from their homelands, some of their ancient practices and ways of life are being lost. The people would like to go home and start rebuilding their lives and communities. Whether this desire can be fulfilled, however, depends on a political compromise being reached by the north and the south that will take into account the differing and often diametrically opposed political and religious interests of the two regions.

AN INTRICATE AND VARIED LANDSCAPE

The North African nation of Sudan, with an area of about 967,000 square miles, is the largest country in terms of land on the African continent. Sudan's significance is enhanced by the fact that it shares borders with nine other African countries: Egypt to the north; Libya to the northwest; Chad and the Central African Republic to the west; Kenya, Uganda, and the Democratic Republic of the Congo(formerly Zaire) to the south; and Ethiopia and Eritrea to the east. To the northeast of Sudan lies the Red Sea, and just across this narrow body of water lie Saudi Arabia, Yemen, Jordan, and Israel.

With such a vast land area, Sudan is a nation with an intricate and varied landscape containing virtually every type of climatic condition imaginable. In the far north are vast stretches of extremely arid land made up of the Libyan and the Nubian deserts. In the central portion of the country lies the semiarid savanna. The south is made up of swamps and lush tropical forests, and at its eastern, southern, and western borders lie mountain ranges, some with peaks over ten thousand feet high.

THE NORTHERN DESERT
Northern Sudan, dominated by long stretches of the Nubian and the Libyan deserts, is to the minds of some observers perhaps the most impressive region of the country. These extremely dry lands extend from the border with Egypt south almost to Khartoum, west to its border with Chad, and east to the Red Sea. One can see for miles across the sandy, rocky plains, which are spotted by sand dunes—reminders of the fierce sandstorms that frequently occur in the region during the months of May and June. The desert lands account for roughly 30 percent of Sudan and are growing larger every year. It is estimated that Sudan loses about two miles of its land to the encroaching desert annually.

The land, though beautiful to the view, is hot, dry and hostile. Annual rainfall ranges from none along the Egyptian border to about four inches to the north of Khartoum. Temperatures in the north can run as high as 120 degrees Fahrenheit. Along the Nile River and the smaller waterways that feed into it, the land can sustain some crops. Very few Sudanese live in this area. The most populated part of the deseret is along the coastline of the Red Sea, where proximity to this relatively large body of water means there is more rainfall and slightly lower daytime temperatures.

THE SEMI-ARID CENTRAL REGION

South and west of the desert region is the rolling, sandy plain of central Sudan. Greater rainfall—ranging from eight inches in the plain's northern edge and increasing to thirty inches going south—makes it possible to grow a variety of crops, such as sorghum, millet, peanuts, sesame seeds, wheat, and cotton, the latter being Sudan's major export crop grown in the area known as the Gezira. The central plain also

Sudan's vast and varied landscape includes arid plains like this, semi-arid savanna, lush tropical forests, and high mountains.

contains stretches of rich grasslands that provide adequate grazing for the cattle and camels owned by the nomadic and seminomadic peoples who make their home in this region.

THE SUDD

Sudan's southern region is dominated by a vast marshland called the Sudd (Arabic for barrier). The Sudd is created by the Nile and other smaller rivers, which run off the slopes of the east African mountains into an enormously wide, shallow basin. The Sudd is aptly named. Choked by nearly impenetrable beds of reeds, papyrus, and other water plants and infested with crocodiles and hippos, the Sudd long served as a natural barrier protecting those who live in the south from invaders from the north. From the earliest times, slavers and armies bent on conquest would find the Sudd's marshy ground too soft for walking and the maze of shallow streams unnavigable. Swarms of insects, such as mosquitoes and tsetse flies, would spread disease among any who tried to move through the area. "Only the dogged, and the luckiest travelers" ever made it alive through the Sudd, says author Rowlinson Carter. Early travelers considered it "a most frightful place."[2]

Northern Sudan's deserts are hot, dry, and virtually uninhabitable.

However, the presence of water year-round and the warm climate make farming possible along the edges of the Sudd.

Crops include maize, groundnuts, sesame, cassava, sweet potatoes, tobacco, and cotton. Livestock, such as goats and sheep, do well, as do fowl, such as chickens. The forests provide game and wild fruits in abundance. The rivers are great sources of fish, which both supplement the diet of the local people and are exported to the neighboring countries to the south.

Despite the productivity of the lands bordering the Sudd, life in these areas is hardly easy. Floods frequently destroy crops and homes; mosquitoes and tsetse flies that historically helped deter invaders also plague the local people. In addition, insects spread diseases, such as sleeping sickness, which kills cattle and immobilizes humans.

The Tropical South

South of the Sudd is the tropical rain forest. It covers about 250,000 square miles, which is nearly 25 percent of the total land area of Sudan. It extends from the Sudd south to the border with Uganda and the Central African Republic. In sharp contrast to the extremely arid north, rainfall here ranges from thirty to sixty inches in the southernmost reaches of the country. Vegetation consists of thick, tall grass, and woodlands where many tropical trees, as well as wildlife, including elephants, are abundant. The many rivers and streams found here are home to crocodiles, hippos, and a variety of fish.

The Mountains

Complementing Sudan's diverse landscape are the highlands and mountain ranges that border the country to the east, west, and south. In addition, in west-central Sudan are found the distinctive Nuba Mountains. These are scattered granite masses rising as high as three thousand feet above the flat clay plain and are covered in many areas by different varieties of savanna vegetation. The valleys between the hills contain numerous wells and streams, allowing for the cultivation of many crops.

At the eastern border, toward the Red Sea, are found the Red Sea hills where the highest peak rises above seven thousand feet. The region is rich in timber, such as teak, mahogany, and eucalyptus, and other natural resources, such as gold, which has been mined in the area since the earliest of times.

PAPYRUS

One of the dominating features of the Sudd is the tall and sturdy papyrus palm that thrives in the swampy waters. It grows to about ten feet high and has long, woody roots that spread under the surface of the water, anchoring the plant. Its thick and spreading fibrous roots are one reason the Sudd is difficult to navigate.

The papyrus is a highly valuable plant: paper and paper products are made from it; its roots are dried and used for fuel; and the pith in the stem is boiled and eaten.

The western border contains the Jebel Mountains. These are distinctive, rounded pillars of rock that stand out over the lower wooded slopes. The mountain valleys have rich fertile soil, and this, combined with frequent rainfall, make the region agriculturally productive. The highest peak in the range is an extinct volcano called Gimbala, which rises to 10,079 feet. Gimbala is home to hot springs, waterfalls, and mountain pools.

To the south, close to the border with Uganda, are the Imatong and Dingotona mountains. The Imatongs are the highest mountains in Sudan, with peaks rising to about 10,000 feet, including Sudan's highest peak, Mount Kinyeti, at 10,460 feet. These mountains receive as much as sixty inches of rain annually, so they are blanketed with thick forests and tall grasses.

THE NILE RIVER

Of all geographical features of the country, none is more significant to Sudan than the Nile River. There would be little life in much of Sudan without the Nile and its tributaries. The Nile and the smaller rivers that feed into it form the focal point of most settlements. Communities in Sudan's desert region depend entirely on the Nile for water, and in the south and central plains, nomads frequently rely on the Nile to water their livestock. Furthermore, any significant agricultural enterprise in the country is irrigated by water drawn from the Nile.

Apart from providing water for farming and consumption by people and animals, the Nile contains many different species of fish that provide nourishment to the Sudanese.

These include perch, salmon, catfish, and tiger fish. Fish, especially perch, are so plentiful that some are preserved and exported.

More than four thousand miles long, the Nile is the longest river in the world; its course through Sudan alone is more than two thousand miles. For much of its course through

©1994 MAGELLAN Geographix℠Santa Barbara, CA (800) 929-4627

Sudan, however, the Nile is really two rivers—the White Nile and the Blue Nile. These two waterways arise from two different sources. Geographers consider the White Nile's source—the starting point in measuring the river's length—to be Lake Victoria, which is shared by the central African nations of Uganda, Kenya, and Tanzania. From where it first enters Sudan at Nimule, the White Nile flows sluggishly for about a hundred miles through the tropical woodland to Juba and continues north to Gondokoro. The river at this point is full of floating, decaying lumps of plant matter, which according to Carter makes the White Nile resemble "a stream of little cabbages bobbing [up and] down."[3]

From Gondokoro the river gains speed, becoming a series of unnavigable rapids after which it empties into the vast and swampy Sudd. It then becomes a series of channels meandering through thick beds of reeds and mud banks. North of the Sudd, the river winds for about four hundred miles and is then joined by the Bahr al-Ghazal and the Sobat Rivers,

A herd of cattle crosses the Nile River. The Nile's course across Sudan is more than two thousand miles long.

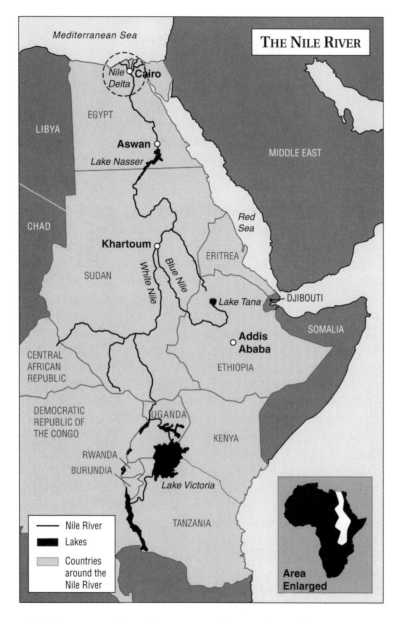

which in turn collect the waters of several smaller rivers. The White Nile then flows sluggishly for another six hundred miles to Khartoum, the capital of Sudan, where its other main tributary, the Blue Nile, joins it.

The Blue Nile rises from Lake Tana in the Ethiopian highlands to the east. Its course is shorter, swifter, and more turbulent than the White Nile. The Blue Nile enters Sudan through a gorge that is almost a mile deep in places and flows northwest for about five hundred miles through the Sudan plains to join the White Nile. At their junction at Khartoum, the two rivers flow northward through the desert region of northern Sudan. About two hundred miles north of Khartoum, the Nile is joined by the waters of the Atbara, its last tributary. It then winds its way through Dongola and Wadi Halfa to the Egyptian border, from which it continues its course to the Mediterranean.

CLIMATE

The central feature of Sudan's climate is heat. K.M. Barbour, author of *The Republic of the Sudan: A Regional Geography*, states that "there is no part of the country where the sun does not pass directly overhead at some time of the year."[4] As a result, average daily temperatures range from 84 to 120 degrees Fahrenheit, depending on the season and the region. Temperatures in the south stay relatively the same all year round with average temperatures at 85 degrees Fahrenheit. Humidity increases during the rainy season, from April to October, and can make the heat feel oppressive.

Unlike in the south, the climate is less humid in the north, and the temperature varies according to the season. The dry season, from November until March, features cooler temperatures with daytime averages at 84 degrees Fahrenheit. The nights are cooler and pleasant at about 72 degrees Fahrenheit. The wet season, from April to October, is hot, with temperatures reaching as high as 120 degrees Fahrenheit. Relief comes only with the brief rains that fall during these months. In the far north there is almost no relief from the intense heat because no rain falls in the region.

Sudan's environment is one of extremes. In the desert north there is almost no water, except that which comes from the Nile, while flooding is not uncommon in the south. Also, both the northern and central regions experience severe sandstorms, which the people call haboob. The haboob is quite predictable, as it usually occurs after a stifling, windless hot spell. According to Barbour:

> a wall of yellow dust is seen approaching, often from the east or north east and then the storm arrives, the wind speed rises to gale force, and for an hour or more

the air is filled with flying dust, to a height of several thousand of feet. Eventually the wind abates, rain falls, bringing a fall in temperature and the dust is temporarily laid.[5]

The haboob occurs anytime between March and October, but is most frequent from May to July. During the haboob, all activities come to a stop, since outdoors, people experience severe sight and respiratory problems, and dust particles clog air intakes on cars and other vehicles and work their way into machinery of all kinds.

NATURAL RESOURCES

Sudan is blessed with a wealth of natural resources, most of them undeveloped. For example, it has only recently begun to take advantage of its oil reserves, currently producing 185,000 barrels per day, although geologists estimate the reserves could yield as much as 600,000 barrels per day. The country also has large deposits of natural gas (estimated at 3 million cubic feet) and other mineral deposits, such as iron, copper, chromium, zinc, tungsten, mica, silver, and gold.

Perhaps the greatest natural resource, however, is the Nile, which is a potential source of hydroelectric energy. Nonetheless, only two dams have been built inside Sudan's borders. Lack of planning resulted in the displacement of whole communities as river valleys were flooded, making construction of the dams controversial. Also, environmentalists see dams as great threats to marine life and wildlife. Some in Sudan hope, however, that with careful planning and thorough research, this aspect of Sudan's natural resources can be utilized to the great benefit of the country.

MAJOR CITIES AND TOWNS

Even though most Sudanese still live in rural areas, Sudan has some of the fastest growing cities in Africa. Frequent droughts, flooding, and ongoing civil war in the the south cause many people to move to the cities. The major cities include El Faher (52,000), Atbara (110,000), Wadi Medani (185,000), Kassala (100,000), Juba (57,000), Port Sudan (230,000), and Khartoum with a population of 2 million, making it the largest and most important city in Sudan.

KHARTOUM

Khartoum is more than Sudan's capital city. With its suburbs of North Khartoum and Omdurman, Khartoum serves as the industrial, commercial, and intellectual center of Sudan. It is home to many industries, including hide tanning, gum processing, textiles, glass, food processing, and printing, as well as many educational and cultural institutions.

Khartoum, quite appropriately, is situated at almost the geographical center of the country. Khartoum in Arabic means "Elephant's Trunk," a reference to the way the Blue Nile on a map appears to curve up and away from the city in the same way an elephant trunk curves up and away from the body. The climate in Khartoum is hot, although the humidity is low. The most severe heat occurs in May, June, and July, with temperatures reaching as high as 109 degrees

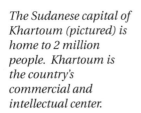

The Sudanese capital of Khartoum (pictured) is home to 2 million people. Khartoum is the country's commercial and intellectual center.

Fahrenheit on any given day. The coolest days are in January, with temperatures of about 87 degrees Fahrenheit. Average rainfall is about four inches, falling between June and September.

PORT SUDAN

After Khartoum, Port Sudan—with a population of approximately 230,000—is Sudan's second most important commercial center. Located on the Red Sea coast, it has a modern harbor and serves as the country's only port. Ships from Port Sudan call at other Red Sea ports in neighboring countries and at Mediterranean and northern European ports as well. Port Sudan serves as the nation's prime export center for cotton, peanuts, oil, skins, and hides. An oil refinery and an international airport are located near the city. The country's major railway has a terminal in the city also.

Sudan's varied and intricate landscape, although not without its challenges, offers great potential for the Sudanese as they build their nation's prosperity. More difficult to overcome is the challenge of creating a sense of unified purpose in a nation consisting of many peoples who often see themselves in competition with one another.

2

THE SUDANESE PEOPLE

Sudan is home to more than 150 different ethnic groups, each numbering from as many as 10 million people to as few as five hundred. Each group has its own language, history, customs, and way of life. Often the differences between ethnic groups, especially the Arabs of the north and the black Africans of the south, have been a source of conflict that has brought hardship and destruction to the lives of many. Yet the different customs and ways of life enrich the culture of Sudan, helping make it one of the most culturally fascinating places in the world.

Historians and anthropologists speak of Sudan as being divided into two major regions—north and south. The boundaries of these regions are both geographical and cultural, with the result that members of the ethnic groups living in the north and the central areas as far south as the Sudd have more in common with each other than they have with peoples living south of the Sudd, and whose lands extend to Sudan's borders with the east African nations of Kenya, Uganda, and the Democratic Republic of the Congo.

Northern and central Sudan is home to many ethnic groups, most of whom have in common their adherence to varying forms of the Islamic faith and their claim to Arab ancestry. The northerners fall into one of two major categories based on their lifestyles—the nomads, who make their living from traveling through Sudan and raising their animals, and the non-nomadic groups. The major non-nomadic groups include the Arabs, the Nubians, the Nuba, the Beja, and the Fur.

ARABS

The largest ethnic group in the north, as well as in Sudan as a whole, is the Arabs. They comprise roughly 39 percent of the Sudanese population. Members of this group, descendants of Arab merchants, nomads, and soldiers who migrated to Sudan around the seventh century consider themselves Arabs, although their ancestors intermarried with the native Nubians and adopted many Nubian customs. Sudanese Arabs honor their heritage by their strict adherence to Islam and their use of the Arabic language. Most, about 99 percent, belong to the Sunni branch of Islam. Many live and work in the cities and towns of the north, although a few are farmers. Some, though very few, still lead strictly the same nomadic existence as their ancestors led. Because of their numeric strength and the historic events during the country's colonial era, Sudanese Arabs dominate their nation's government.

NUBIANS

While the Arabs thrived and became Sudan's largest ethnic group, the Nubians, who were already in Sudan when the Arabs arrived, still comprise the second largest ethnic group in the north. They number about 4 million, roughly 8 percent of the Sudanese population. Nubians are descendants of a people who in ancient times lived along the banks of the Nile in the far north of Sudan, mostly within a hundred miles of

Sudanese Arabs like this man comprise approximately 39 percent of the country's population.

Sudan's second largest ethnic group, Nubians like this young woman are descendants of the country's earliest inhabitants.

the Egyptian border. However, in 1964, their original homeland was flooded when Egypt completed work on the Aswan High Dam, forming a large body of water known as Lake Nasser. The flooding of their homeland forced many Sudanese Nubians to relocate to Khashm al-Girba or Wadi Halfa, nearly five hundred miles (approximately eight hundred kilometers) away from their ancestral home.

Nubians are mostly farmers, growing cotton in the Atbara River valley. A few, however, migrated to the cities, where they generally find jobs as taxi drivers or operate small shops. Nubian farmers, when not occupied by other chores, engage in handicrafts, especially those related to farming, such as constructing waterwheels, which are used to draw water from the Nile to irrigate the fields. Waterwheels are turned by oxen, and young boys are assigned the job of keeping the oxen on task.

Today, the Nubians, like the Sudanese Arabs, are Muslim, although they have maintained some of the rituals predating their conversion to Islam. These include several rites-of-passage ceremonies, such as naming, birth, male and female circumcision, marriage, and death ceremonies.

NUBA

Just as the Nubians can trace their presence in Sudan to ancient times, so too can the Nuba, who—despite the similarity in name—are a distinct ethnic group. The Nuba, five hundred thousand strong, live in the mountains of west-central Sudan, in the Nuba Mountains, and trace their heritage to the Cushites, a people who lived in the Nile River valley as early as 3200 B.C. The Cushites, around 2400 B.C., developed the first Sudanese Empire, which lasted for many centuries before being conquered by invaders from Ethiopia in A.D. 350. Today, Nuba are mostly farmers. Like Nubians, Nuba practice a modified version of Islam under which they keep some of their ancient customs, including the eating of pork, which is forbidden by Islam.

Traditional Nuba homes, in which people live in large, extended family groups, are distinctive. The houses, called *tukls*, are round mud structures, with a cone-shaped, thatched roof. In the family compounds, each *tukl* is connected to the others by mud walls. Each compound often consists of five or more *tukls* built to form a circular complex. The entrance to each *tukl* is a keyhole-shaped opening in the middle, usually about four feet from the ground. Several compounds cluster together to form a community.

THE NUBA AND THE SUDANESE CIVIL WAR

The Sudanese civil war has had a devastating impact on the life of the Nuba. Their insistence on keeping their traditional customs has resulted in conflict with profundamentalist Islamic groups. As a result, many Nuba have been killed and many deported from their homeland in the hills to government-run "peace villages," were they are forced to adopt a more conservative form of the Islamic faith or join the government troops fighting the southern rebels. Many have receded well into the hills to protect themselves from the raids and fighting; others have migrated to neighboring counties as refugees. In all these forced movements, the traditional way of life that the Nuba struggle to maintain is disappearing.

Nuba houses blend well with their natural surroundings and are well suited to the local climate. Thanks to the mud walls that naturally regulate temperatures, the houses are warm during the cooler rainy season; conversely, they are cool during the hot, dry season. A man builds one *tukl* for his wife upon marriage; the wife does not come to live with him until the house is built.

BEJA

A people with an equally ancient claim to Sudan as the Nuba are the Beja, who live in the northeastern part of Sudan between the Red Sea and the Nile River. Beja—now numbering more than eight hundred thousand—are thought to have been a nomadic people who left their homeland in the Arabian Peninsula and eventually settled about five thousand years ago in what today is Sudan.

Originally animists, Beja converted to Christianity during the sixth century, the result of influence from Christians in nearby Ethiopia. But during the next century, when Muslim Arabs arrived in Sudan, many Beja converted to Islam. By the fourteenth century, the majority of Beja were Muslim. Today the Beja are primarily Muslim. They speak their native tongues (Beja or To Bedawi and Tigrinya) as well as Arabic.

Even though their ancestors were nomads, most Beja have adopted a settled lifestyle. Many are farmers, growing cotton and grain in the fertile areas of the Red Sea hills and along the Gash watercourses. The development of Port Sudan into a busy commercial center also has opened opportunities to the Beja, who find employment in the docks. By custom, Beja do not eat fish, although some work in the lucrative fishing industries in the areas processing fish for export to other countries. Other Beja still raise cattle as their ancestors did, and sell the meat in Port Sudan both for local consumption and export.

FUR

As numerous as the Beja, but living in the northwest of Sudan in the region known as Darfur (Arabic for Land of the Fur), are the Fur. Darfur is a highland region dominated by the volcanic mountain slopes of the Jebel Mountains. The Fur are concentrated in the mountainous heartland of the province, although many reside in El Fasher—a town lying to

AFRICAN TRADITIONAL RELIGION

African indigenous religion, also called animism, consists of belief in the existence of a higher power or Supreme Being. In southern Sudan, the different ethnic groups have different names for this male being, according to their language. For the Dinka, he is called Dengdit or Nyalich; for the Shilluk, he is called Juok. Under the Supreme Being are different gods, less powerful than the Supreme Being but more powerful than humans. These gods are said to control the natural order and require worship from their followers as well as strict adherence to natural laws. It is believed that the gods can bring blessings or disasters upon their followers, depending on how faithfully the followers adhere to natural laws. The natural world is given to humans to use in providing for their daily needs, but humans may not misuse or waste any part of it. As such, the goal of animists is to maintain harmony with the natural laws by observing stipulated rituals and social behavior.

There is also belief in ancestral spirits who are said to play very significant roles in the lives of the people. The ancestral spirits are not gods. They live in the spirit world, and through the powers they possess as part of living in the spirit world, they can protect family members from harm as well as intercede on behalf of their family members before the gods. Living family members are required to observe certain religious rituals in recognition of the dead ancestors, including respecting and acknowledging their presence during important family meetings, even though the living cannot see them, and pouring libation in their honor during family and community ceremonies. In some communities, it is also believed that the spirits of the ancestors come back in successive generations of rainmakers or spiritual chiefs who serve as authority figures.

the northeast of the mountainous region. El Fasher was once of strategic importance for the control of routes used by traders and Muslim pilgrims on their way to Mecca.

The Fur traditionally traded in ebony, ivory, spices, rich cloth, other goods, and slaves. Today, however, while many still engage in trade, others are farmers, growing food for their own use and to be sold in the markets. Crops include vegetables and grains such as corn and millet—the latter used by the Fur to make a variety of food dishes and drinks.

Like other peoples of the north, the majority of Fur are Muslim, although they still practice some of their pre-Islamic rituals, such as rainmaking and marriage ceremonies.

NOMADIC PEOPLES OF THE NORTH

An estimated 20 percent of Sudanese are nomads, living mostly in the northern and central plains and around the western and eastern mountains, where the grasslands provide grazing for their cattle. Emil Ludwig, writer and traveler to Sudan, says "only a nomad can be a master of the desert and the plain, for to live on his herds, he must lead them from pasture to pasture, following the vagaries of the climate and the river, and above all, the belts of rain."[6] Like the majority of the northern peoples, the nomads are predominantly Muslim. Nomadic groups include the Falasha, Zaghawa, and the Baggara. The Baggara, at 1 million people, are by far the most numerous.

The nomads of Sudan travel across the central and northern plains of the country by camel, driving their herds of cattle from pasture to pasture.

BAGGARA

Baggara speak a variant of Arabic and are descended from Bedouin nomads who are said to have migrated from across the Red Sea, in Saudi Arabia, between the eleventh and the fourteenth centuries. By the eighteenth century, the Baggara were settled in their present homeland in central and western Sudan and had intermarried with the local peoples. Baggara are cattle herders and consider cattle as central to their existence. The name Baggara comes from the Arabic word *bagar*, which means "cow." The dream of every Baggara man is

CATTLE

In nomadic or seminomadic communities, the cow is a cherished possession and central to the people's way of life. A family's status is determined by the number of cattle it owns. Cattle provide for a wide variety of material needs. Cow's milk is drunk or made into butter, which in turn can be made into oil for cooking or moisturizing the skin. Among the Dinka, cattle urine is used for washing, dyeing hair, and tanning hides. The dung is used as fuel; the smoke from dung fires repels insects, and the ash is used as insect repellent, for body decoration, and its fine abrasive quality makes it a good cleaning agent.

If an animal dies—usually through old age or an accident—every part of it is put to use. The skins are made into leather for mats, drums, cloth, and ropes; the meat is eaten; and the horns and bones can be carved into tools or musical instruments.

Because of the importance of the cattle to such large numbers of Sudanese, many ascribe great religious and social importance to them. Cattle are sacrificed in religious worship, are used to make payments that settle disputes, and to seal alliances. They are also given as bride wealth to legally confirm a marriage.

to own large herds of cattle, as many as several thousand since in their society this means greater wealth and prestige for the individual. However, only a very few Baggara can boast of such an achievement; the majority own between two or three hundred head of cattle.

Baggara live part of the year on the northern margins of the Sudd, but move in response to the changing seasons. They plant some crops at the beginning of summer. During the summer months, however, as the rainfall gets heavier, mosquitoes and tsetse flies flourish in the Sudd, forcing the men to move their herds farther north. The women and children stay behind to continue cultivating the crops and then move north to join the men. Later, when the northern grasslands become parched, the Baggara move back to their homesteads to harvest their crops, mostly cotton and sorghum. During the driest part of the year, they move even farther south. By this time, the mosquitoes and flies have mostly died and the Baggara's herds find ample grass on which to feed.

Because they are constantly on the move, Baggara live mostly in tents that are easily dismantled. The tents, which are usually round with cone-shaped roofs, are made of available materials. Tree branches and sticks cut from vegetation around their campsites make the basic framework, then strips of bark, mats, plastic sheeting, or cowhides are arranged to cover this framework. A rope is tied around the structure to keep it secure.

According to custom, a Baggara man may have up to four wives, in keeping with the teachings of Islam. But his first wife must be a cousin, preferably a father's brother's daughter. This custom serves to maintain family unity, as it keeps most members of the extended family together in one place and in close contact with each other. The groom pays the dowry for his wife in cattle. Money obtained from the dowry is used to purchase many of the possessions the bride will need in her new home, including clothes, linens, pots, blankets, and other household items. Islam requires that wives all be supported and treated equally, and not every Baggara man can afford to have more than one wife as a result. However, in polygamous homes, each wife owns her own dwelling, which she operates independently.

PEOPLES OF THE SOUTH

Like the north, the south of Sudan is home to diverse ethnic groups. What the southern peoples have in common, and what sets them apart from the northern Sudanese, is that none of them claim Arab ancestry and the majority are not

 ## ISLAM

The majority of Sudanese people who live in the north are Muslim. They believe in one god, Allah, and consider Muhammad to be his prophet. Central to every Muslim's belief are the Five Pillars of Faith, which comprise the framework for living:

1. Belief in Allah and his prophet, Muhammad.
2. Pray five times a day, facing east, the direction of the holy city of Mecca.
3. Give alms to the poor.
4. Observe the month of Ramadan.
5. Visit Mecca at least once in one's lifetime, if possible.

Muslim. The various ethnic groups number from as many as 1 million to as few as one hundred. They are said to have migrated from neighboring Kenya, Uganda, and the Lake Chad region from the fifteenth through the seventeenth centuries. Some of the ethnic groups still have members in the regions from which they long ago migrated. Major ethnic groups include the Dinka, Shilluk, Nuer, and Azande. Except for the Azande, who are mostly settled farmers, the rest of the people are seminomads, combining animal herding with farming.

DINKA

Dinka are the largest ethnic group in the south, numbering over 1 million. They are divided into twenty different clans, each consisting of from roughly thirty thousand to sixty thousand members. Each clan is an extended family whose members form their own political and religious hierarchy independent of the other groups. The leader of each clan, called the *beng*, is an elder chosen by other elders and family heads in the community. The *beng* is charged with providing political and spiritual leadership for the clan, including performing religious ceremonies and rituals, providing advice in times of difficulties, and settling disputes. He also has the power to represent and speak for his clan in the larger Dinka community.

The region where the Dinka live is mostly grass-covered uplands with scattered trees and shrubs, which slopes down to the Sudd. In such an environment, the Dinka are able to combine cattle raising with subsistence farming. Much like nomads, they organize their lives according to the season. During the rainy season, from April to October, they live in permanent settlements where they grow different types of crops, such as wheat, corn, millet, and vegetables, including pumpkins and okra. When the Sudd floods in midsummer and the region is infested with tsetse flies and other insects, the young men take the cattle to drier ground for pasture, leaving the rest of the people to tend to the crops. When the floods subside in early September, the young herders return home to help with the harvest.

Following the harvest, before the dry season really sets in, the Dinka have a little leisure time. This is a time when many festivals are held and marriages are arranged. Many Dinka also spend time fishing in the slowly receding rivers. The fish

Dinka villagers water their cattle. The Dinka are the largest ethnic group in southern Sudan.

that are not eaten right away are sun dried and sold in the markets. As the dry season advances, the settlements are practically abandoned as the people move closer to the rivers where new grass feeds the livestock. Only the elderly and mothers who are nursing are left behind to take care of the homes.

While a few Dinka are Christians, the majority adhere to the indigenous religion of their ancestors, which includes belief in many gods.

NUER

Like the Dinka, the Nuer are a seminomadic group who share the same homeland with the Dinka. Also like the Dinka, they structure their lives around the seasons, moving upland with their herds when the Sudd is flooded during the rainy season and returning to harvest their crops when the floods subside. In addition, like the Dinka, most Nuer still practice their indigenous religion of belief in many gods.

Nuer speak their own language, called Nuer. One can always tell the Nuer from the Dinka by facial scarring: Nuer males and females receive facial scarring during initiation ceremonies into adulthood. The scarring, which follows distinct patterns, is a symbol of Nuer identity. Any Nuer without the facial marking is still considered a child and not a full member of the community.

SHILLUK

Shilluk live still farther south in Sudan, along the banks of the White Nile. There are about 120,000 Shilluk, making them less numerous than the Dinka and the Nuer. Shilluk, unlike the Nuer and the Dinka are sedentary rather than seminomadic. They grow crops along the banks of the Nile and keep

Shilluk men smoke a pipe at their village in southern Sudan. The Shilluk live along the banks of the White Nile.

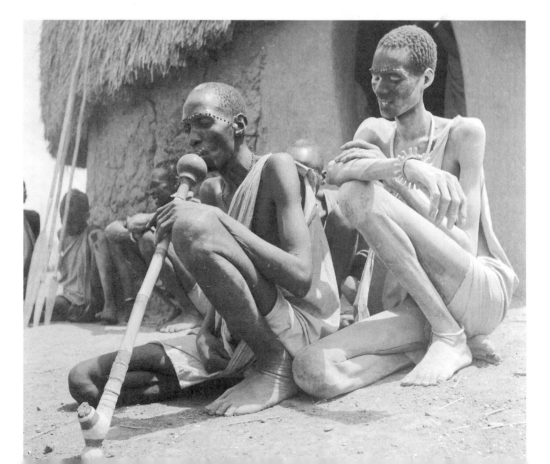

a few domestic animals, such as sheep and goats. Because they live along the banks of the Nile, fishing—an additional source of food—is one of their favorite activities. They speak their native tongue, called Shilluk, and like the other ethnic groups in the south are non-Islamic. They practice ancestral worship and belief in many gods.

The leader of the Shilluk is called a *reth*, who is looked to for both political and religious leadership and is seen as a living symbol of Shilluk history and culture. He is also thought to be possessed by the spirit of Nyikang—the first Shilluk king and cultural hero. Indeed, the *reth*'s role is more religious then political. His subjects believe he is the reincarnation of the legendary Nyikang and that his good health ensures their prosperity.

A *reth* is chosen from members of a single royal family by the elders. The choice is crowned during the coronation ceremony, which every Shilluk attends. At the coronation, it is believed that the new *reth* becomes possessed by the spirit of Nyikang. There is a mock battle after the coronation in which the king symbolically conquers—and is finally accepted by— his people.

Like the Nuer, at the initiation into adulthood the Shilluk are given facial scarring as a mark of ethnic identity. Some of the scarring looks like beads running across the individual's temple.

THE SHILLUK *RETH*

The Shilluk king, called *reth*, is given great honor among his people. Even his own sons must hide their faces and avoid eye contact when addressing him; foreigners address him in a crouched position. While the king lives, he is regarded as bearing within himself the whole life and spirit of his people. He therefore must look after himself, his health, and his well-being very carefully. If he were to become ill or senile, it is believed that this would lead to sickness and death among the cattle, crops, and humans. For this reason, it believed that the community must never have a king who is old and weak. When he becomes incapable of fulfilling his duties, he must "die." In the past, the king simply left his community and wandered into the forest to die. Today he resigns his post so that a new king may be chosen.

AZANDE

Like the Shilluk, the Azande, who live in southwestern Sudan, look to a king for political and religious leadership. The king is chosen from a designated royal clan by community elders and is charged with the welfare of his people. He upholds the people's customs and rituals and presides over important ceremonies, such as marriages and funerals. He also serves as the political spokesperson for his people within the larger Sudanese society.

Also like the Shilluk, the Azande are farmers, growing crops such as corn, millet, sweet potatoes, and peanuts, while raising livestock, such as sheep and goats. Similar to all the southern ethnic groups, the Azande also practice the indigenous African religion of belief in many gods. Their supreme being is Mboli, who is said to be all-powerful. They also believe in witchcraft and that certain people—usually they are men—can practice harmful witchcraft without intending to do so. Therefore, making somebody aware that he is a witch is considered a good thing because it gives the individual a chance to realize what he has been doing in order to make amends and become a good citizen.

Given the tremendous diversity of the religious beliefs, lifestyles, and political leadership, the greatest challenge for the Sudanese is to achieve unity as a nation. While diversity enriches Sudan's culture, it has also served historically as a source of political conflict. Internal squabbles often rendered the Sudanese vulnerable to invasion and domination by outsiders. Throughout Sudan's history, colonial powers reinforced the people's religious and cultural differences, initiating policies that maintained divisions among the Sudanese to the colonists' benefit.

3

A LAND OF EMPIRES AND KINGDOMS

Scholars say that what eventually came to be called Sudan was historically a collection of separate empires, kingdoms, and small city-states. In early times, as it is today, Sudan was sharply divided between north and south. The northern and southern parts of what one day would be Sudan had distinct cultural and political traditions.

THE SMALL CITY-STATES OF SOUTHERN SUDAN

Archeologists believe that people have lived in what today is southern Sudan since as early as 5000 B.C. However, the south's documented history dates back to the fifteenth century when the Dinka left their homeland in the eastern lake region of Uganda and migrated north. Over time, the Dinka displaced the original inhabitants, of whom little is known.

In the two centuries following the Dinka's arrival, other peoples, such as the Shilluk, Nuer, and Azande, arrived. As they fought with the Dinka and among themselves for land and food, these groups organized themselves into independent communities with formal political and spiritual structures that still survive today.

From the very beginning, contact between the peoples in the south with those to the north was less than friendly. Even though there is evidence of some cultural and political interaction between north and south, the relationship between the two regions consisted mostly of raids by slave traders from the north. Northerners primarily viewed the dark-skinned peoples of the south as potential slaves to be used as domestic servants in the northern homes or exported to Egypt for use as laborers, domestic servants, concubines, or soldiers. The hostility these raids caused would be passed down from one generation to the next. The south today still looks to the north as would-be oppressors.

THE NORTHERN KINGDOMS

Whereas scholars know relatively little about ancient peoples of southern Sudan, they know a great deal about the history of northern Sudan, thanks to stories told by historians living in ancient Egypt of their nation's relations with its neighbors to the south. The earliest recorded history points to the people known as Cushites who settled along the Nile River in the eastern part of the country around 3200 B.C. Some scholars argue that the Cushites were part of the Egyptian Empire originally, but began to assert their independence around 2400 B.C. According to this theory, by 2000 B.C., Cush had achieved complete independence from Egypt. The Cush Kingdom covered much of what is today southern Egypt and northern Sudan, extending as far south as the confluence of the Blue Nile and the White Nile.

The ancestors of this Nuer man arrived in southern Sudan hundreds of years ago.

THE KINGDOM OF CUSH

The kingdom of Cush was rich in natural resources, such as gold, iron, and other metals, and precious stones. Sustained by irrigation from the Nile floodwaters, Cush also prospered from agriculture and, for centuries, engaged in trade with neighboring countries, especially Egypt and Ethiopia, exchanging gold, ivory, wood, and slaves acquired from the interior country for needed items such as cotton.

Cush's wealth was both a blessing and a curse. The Cushites lived well, but their wealth tempted Egypt's kings to make frequent attempts to control Cush and its resources. Eventually, around 1500 B.C.,

PIANKHY

From 751 to 712 B.C. Piankhy was the Nubian king of Cush. He was the son of Kashta, the first Nubian king to gain independence from Egypt and wage war for the control of the country. Piankhy completed the military campaign begun by his father and ruled Egypt until his death in 721. He was a brilliant and fierce general, and there are many stories about his military successes. The carved stone slab commemorating his conquests was found near the great temple of Amen Re' in 1862 and is now in the Cairo Museum. Although Piankhy was in full control of Egypt during his lifetime, he did not directly rule Egypt. He was satisfied with receiving tributes from the princes as the king of Cush and Egypt. At his death, his brother, Shabaka, became king and established direct control over the two countries, moving his capital from Napata to Thebes in Egypt. The Cushites would rule Egypt for two more generations before being defeated by the invading Assyrian army. The Cushites then retreated to their home in Sudan to fortify it against the Assyrians.

Egypt took control of Cush, and subsequently Egyptian officials, priests, merchants, and artisans came to settle in the region. These Egyptian immigrants introduced their culture and ways of life to the Cushites. They built temples and pyramids, imposed Egyptian laws, and taught the Cushites how to use hieroglyphics, the ancient Egyptian form of writing.

The Cushites refused to accept Egyptian domination, however, and under the leadership of their king, Kashata, regained control of their kingdom in 751 B.C. Kashata was not satisfied with regaining Cush's independence, however, and launched a military campaign against Egypt, moving north to take over southern Egypt. At his death in 740 B.C. his successor, Piankhy, effected the complete takeover of Egypt, establishing Egypt's Twenty-fifth Dynasty. Cushite kings then proceeded to rule Egypt for the next seventy-five years.

Cush lost Egypt to Assyria in 657 B.C. With the loss of Egypt, the then-king of Cush, Tanwetamani, and his forces were forced to retreat to their kingdom's former border. The Cushites, then, paid greater attention to their borders, fortifying them against the Assyrians whose military power they feared.

THE MOVE TO MEROE

One of the defensive measures the Cushite kings took in protecting the country from the Assyrians was to move their capital from Napata, which was close to the northern boundary and considered vulnerable, to Meroe, between the Blue Nile and the Atbara. The move to Meroe was completed in 538 B.C. and proved its value strategically. From their new capital, Cush's rulers expanded their kingdom southward and westward to include present-day regions of Darfur and Korfordan in central Sudan. Meroe's location afforded Cush's kings with access to many resources, including good land for grazing and sources of iron ore. "Iron ore," according to archaeologist P.L. Shinnie, "was easily available in the ironstone formation which caps the sandstone hills over much of northern Sudan and in quantity in the Island of Meroe."[7] These resources would enable Meroe to emerge as a wealthy,

The crumbling pyramids at Meroe serve as testament to the once-powerful Cushite civilization.

LIVES OF ANCIENT NUBIANS

Among the first people to live in what today is Sudan were the Nubians. Excavations of ancient sites, especially burial chambers of their kings and queens, continue to reveal the Nubian lifestyle. The earliest tombs date from 400 to 300 B.C. and were buried under mounds of earth from seven to forty feet high. They also contain a wealth of treasures, such as gold and silver jewelry, silverware and ironware, and many bronze articles including folding tables and chairs. The presence of imported goods from Greece, Rome, and Egypt confirms the influence of the Nubian civilization and their contact with other ancient civilizations.

vibrant city, like Napata, and to become an important center for learning and commerce.

For all its prosperity, however, Cush began to decline by the turn of the millennium as it came under repeated attacks from Egypt to the north and Ethiopia to the southeast. In A.D. 350, Cush suffered a great defeat by the Ethiopians and gradually disintegrated into three smaller, but powerful, kingdoms.

THE NUBIAN KINGDOMS OF MAQURRA, ALWA, AND ALODIA

The three kingdoms that emerged following the defeat of Cush are referred to as the Nubian Kingdoms of Maqurra (Makurra or Makuria), Alwa, and Alodia (Nobatia). The kingdom of Alodia was the most northern, covering an area that is part of modern-day southern Egypt. The territory of the second kingdom, Maqurra, extended from Old Dongola near the current Egyptian border, inland to Atbara. Alwa was located south of Maqurra, with its territory extending to just south of modern-day Khartoum where the Blue Nile and White Nile meet. Its capital was Suba (Soba), on the banks of the Blue Nile. In A.D. 632, Alodia and Maqurra combined to form one kingdom, known as al-Maqurra.

The Nubian kingdoms resisted invasion and foreign interference in their internal affairs for centuries. However, as a result of the Egyptian influence, by the early sixth century, the kingdoms gradually converted to Christianity, which had gained dominance in Egypt in A.D. 540. The Coptic Christian church would dominate Nubia for the next six centuries, reaching its height of prosperity around the ninth and tenth centuries. However, another faith introduced into the region by Arab immigrants was by this point gaining in popularity.

THE COMING OF THE ARABS AND ISLAM

As early as the seventh century, Arab nomadic groups had migrated into northern Sudan, mostly the al-Maqurra territory. These Arab nomads were Muslim, but they did not necessarily come out of eagerness to spread their faith: They came in search of pasture for their cattle. In time, however, many Arabs abandoned their nomadic way of life and settled among the local people, with whom they intermarried.

Since inheritance and succession among the Nubians come through the mother's lineage rather than the father's, the descendants of the Arabs, whose mothers were mostly Nubians, were quickly integrated into the lives of their communities. The social acceptance accorded them therefore enabled the Arabs to spread their culture and faith within the community. When the next wave of Arab immigrants arrived during the thirteenth and fourteenth centuries, they would only strengthen the already-established Arab component of the culture, making possible the eventual creation of an Arab and Muslim society.

THE FUNJ (FUNG) EMPIRE

At the same time that the Muslim Arabs were establishing themselves through marriage in the old kingdom of

 CHRISTIANITY IN NUBIA
Nubians were converted to Christianity in the sixth century. Missionaries sent from Constantinople, the capital of the Roman Empire, reached Sudan by way of Egypt around A.D. 540. By the end of the century, Nubian rulers had accepted the faith. The Christian Nubian Kingdom survived for many centuries in spite of external and internal threats. However, it fell during the tenth century as the Muslim influence widened. Remains of castles and churches built during this phase of Sudanese history are still being discovered and studied.

al-Maqurra, Alwa was invaded from the south by a people known as the Funj. The Funj are believed to have been a band of Shilluk raiders who moved north led by their leader Amara Dunqas. By A.D. 910, Dunqas and his followers had conquered some towns and founded a capital at Sennar on the west bank of the Blue Nile, about six miles north of the location of modern-day Sennar. From Sennar, Dunqas and subsequent rulers continued to spread their dominance. By 1400 the Funj had taken over all Alwa territory, extending to somewhere past modern-day Gezira.

For reasons that historians have yet to discover, the Funj rulers converted to Islam by the end of the sixteenth century. Some historians argue that the conversion was a result of increased contact between the Funj and their Muslim neighbors. Sharing a similar faith, it is supposed, would have facilitated trade and political alliances and allowed Funj rulers to wield some political influence with their neighbors. After the conversion to Islam, Funj kings took up the title of sultan. In time, the kingdom came to be described as a black sultanate in recognition of the non-Arab origin of its rulers and the Islamic nature of the political entity they controlled.

Old Sennar straddled a north-south trade route and, as a result, the Funj controlled trading in cloth, dates, and ivory, and slaves obtained in slave raids in the south and in the Nuba Mountains. The Funj remained the most powerful force in central and much of northern Sudan for the next two hundred years until, once again, Egypt—seeking to dominate its neighbor—invaded the whole region north of the Sudd and brought the people there under Egyptian control.

ALI PASHA'S CAMPAIGN

For thousands of years, Egypt had looked to Sudan as a source of slaves and gold. It had obtained these by trading and—when that failed—by raiding. But in 1820, under the leadership of Muhammad Ali Pasha, Egypt invaded and conquered Sudan with the intention of controlling its neighbor completely. A general decline of all three Sudanese kingdoms during the eighteenth century, owing mainly to the deterioration in the quality of rulers, encouraged Ali Pasha to believe that a complete takeover was possible.

The Egyptian force left Cairo in July 1820, four thousand men strong, under the leadership of Muhammad Ali Pasha's

The ivory from elephant tusks, cloth, dates, and slaves were important trade goods in early Sudan.

twenty-five-year-old son, Isma'il Kamil Pasha. It took Isma'il and his army less than a year to gain complete control over northern Sudan, including the old Funj territory. Subsequent expeditions to south and central Sudan brought those regions under Egyptian control as well.

Egypt ruled Sudan for the next sixty years. It brought all the northern territories under one centralized administration and established the seat of government in Khartoum, strategically located at the center of the country. Egyptian-ruled parts of Sudan were run by a governor-general, who reported to Ali Pasha. The duties of the governor-general

GENERAL CHARLES GORDON

In 1877 General Charles Gordon of Britain was appointed governor of Sudan by the Egyptian government, which at the time controlled its southern neighbor. He was the first European to hold such a position. Gordon served until 1880 when he resigned in protest over British actions against the Egyptian government. In his absence, the Sudanese revolution led by Muhammad Ahmad grew in strength. Gordon returned in 1884 to negotiate with the al-Mahdi and quell the revolution. He was unsuccessful. Gordon and his army were surrounded by the Mahdist forces in January 1885, and subsequently massacred.

included overseeing the activities of the local chiefs, collecting taxes, and facilitating trade with Egypt. While most Sudanese disliked and frequently revolted against Egyptian control of their country, their first massive and successful uprising did not occur until 1877. That rebellion, under the leadership of an Islamic teacher by name of Muhammad Ahmad ibnal-Sayyid abd Allah, also known as the Mahdi, lasted for years.

THE MAHDI

In 1881, a religious leader by the name of Muhammad Ahmad ibnal-Sayyid abd Allah announced that he had been called by Allah to return the people to the true practice of Islam and to help rid them of the corrupt Egyptian leadership. His teachings gained him popularity and followers, and the people hailed him as the Mahdi (one who according to Islamic teachings, would one day come to the earth to bring true justice to the world).

The Egyptian leadership, as expected, felt uneasy about the rise of Muhammad Ahmad as a revolutionary leader. Two Egyptian forces were sent into Sudan in 1881 and 1882 respectively to capture the Mahdi. Both failed, however, and the Mahdi and his army, called Ansar, went on the offensive. In 1884 Charles Gordon, a British general working for the Egyptian government, arrived in Sudan to check the Mahdist advance. Gordon offered the Mahdi peace. The offer was rejected, as the Mahdi and his army were sure of defeating the Egyptian troops. On January 26, 1885, the Egyptian garrison at Khartoum, led by Gordon, was attacked by Mahdist forces. Even though the Mahdi had given instructions to his men not to harm Gordon, the general was nonetheless killed when Khartoum fell.

The Mahdi's triumph was short lived, however. He fell ill of typhus and died on June 22, 1885. He was replaced by one of his students, Abdullah ibn Muhammad, who became known as the Khalifa (successor). Under the Khalifa's leadership, the Ansar won many victories in different parts of Sudan. By 1892, the Mahdist state, as it was called, expanded, bringing the whole of northern Sudan under its control. The Khalifa had dreams of carrying his campaign into neighboring countries of Ethiopia and Eritrea, but was checked by the presence of European colonial powers occupying those countries at the time.

Lord Kitchener became governor-general of northern Sudan after the British defeated Muhammad Ahmad's revolutionary army in 1898.

THE COMING OF THE BRITISH

Mahdist control of Sudan began to unravel in 1896 when the British, then in control of Egypt, authorized the Egyptian army to launch a campaign to reconquer Sudan. In March 1896, the newly constituted British and Egyptian army, about 25,800 strong, began its attack on the Mahdist forces. Although the Mahdist. army fought hard, they were eventually defeated in 1898, mostly because the British had better weapons. The defeat of the Ansar by the British and Egyptians paved the way for the next phase of foreign rule in Sudan, the era known as the British-Egyptian rule.

Following Ansar's defeat, the commander of the British

colonial forces in Egypt, Lord Kitchener, became the governor-general of northern Sudan. Kitchener and subsequent governor-generals, however, had to deal with frequent Sudanese uprisings. Still, colonial administrators gradually expanded the territories under their control, despite local opposition. Military expeditions into the Nuba Mountains and to the south, which up to that point had been left alone because the Sudd presented such a formidable obstacle, brought those regions under the control of the British and Egyptians in 1928. So it was that both the northern and southern territories were first brought together as one country, called Sudan.

Despite Britain's creation of a unified country in 1928, Sudan remained divided into two provinces: the north, inhabited by Arabs like this woman, and the south, where various tribes lived.

CONTINUING DIVISIONS

For all practical purposes, however, Sudan remained divided. The colonial administrators governed the two provinces as

they would have ruled two separate nations. In the north, for example, officials made use of the existing institutions in Khartoum, ruling with the help of local bureaucrats. Arabic continued to be the official language of daily life, government transactions, and the educational system. Although the structure of the legal system was modified to reflect British law, it acknowledged local customs and values.

The south posed a greater challenge to the colonial administrators. Unlike in the north, where Arabic was spoken by the majority of the people, the southerners spoke a variety of tribal languages. There was also no dominant culture, nor was there a centralized bureaucracy. Each ethnic group obeyed its own political and spiritual leader, so colonial officials ruled indirectly through these individuals. Daily business and governmental activities were conducted in whatever language was spoken in a particular location. Christian missionaries, however, were allowed to establish schools and to teach English. As a result, over time, English became the common language of government.

Colonial administrators felt that they had to help the southerners preserve their traditional culture and way of life. They did so in part out of fear that increased contact between the north and the south would introduce Islam and Islamic culture in the south. The new converts, colonial officials feared, could then be incited to revolt against the colonists as the Ansar was doing in the north. As a result, officials instituted a closed-door policy in the south that barred northerners from entering or working. Northerners already living and working in the south were asked to leave. The teaching of Islam and Islamic customs, including the wearing of Arab dress, were all made illegal in the south. A 1930 directive stated that the blacks of the southern provinces were to be considered a people distinct from the northern Muslims.

The consequence of isolating the south from the north in this way would prove unhealthy for the political and economic development of the south. Economically, not much was done to develop their natural economic resources. While many projects were initiated in the north to help the northern economy, the south remained untouched. In addition, the missionary schools set up in the south were for the most part ill-equipped and in time proved ineffective for preparing the southerners for full participation in governing the greater Sudan. As independence loomed, the south was at a disadvantage economically and politically. "How different the situation might have been today if a better and foresighted policy of economic and political development had been used in the south,"[8] historian Arnold Toynbee would later remark.

TOWARD INDEPENDENCE

The British colonial practice of employing Sudanese in governing the country fostered the growth of a class of local citizens who had both the experience and the inclination to rule themselves. Beginning in the 1920s, the Sudanese organized into political parties that agitated for independence. However, what an independent Sudan should look like was a matter of debate among the local politicians. Some were nationalists who envisioned a unified north and south; others favored seeing the north as part of Egypt and the south as parts of Uganda and Kenya.

By the 1940s, as the questions about the future of Sudan grew more pressing, there was also increased criticism of the colonial policy of isolating the south. Under pressure from the international community in 1946, Britain agreed to abolish its division of north and south and to administer Sudan as one country. Northerners were allowed to seek employment in the south, and the prohibition against the spread of Islam in the south was lifted. With more and more northerners working in the south, Arabic began to displace English as the language of government.

Southerners who held leadership positions quickly voiced concern about the potential domination of a unified Sudan by northerners. For example, the introduction of Arabic in the south as the language of government put at a disadvantage the southern elites who spoke English, not Arabic. The southern fears intensified in 1953 when an election called to select members of a transitional government clearly favored the north over the south. Of the eight hundred available posts, only four were granted to southerners. For their part, northerners argued that the south had too few qualified candidates to occupy the newly created leadership positions. The hope for a unified, independent country in which both north and south would participate equally seemed to have been shattered by the result of the elections.

Tensions between the south and the northern-dominated government grew, and in 1955, the entire southern military mutinied when their units were placed under the command of northern officers. The rebellious troops killed several hundred northerners. The government quelled the revolt and executed seventy southerners for their role in the uprising. The rest of the rebels fled to remote areas of the south, where they organized armed resistance against the Arab-dominated government. When Sudan was granted independence in January 1956, the new nation's government already had major problems on its hands.

4

Contemporary Sudan

Sudan obtained independence in 1956 without resolving the religious, ethnic, and political differences that had long divided its populace. The consequence has been political instability and a civil war that has raged for all but ten years of the independent nation's existence. Since independence, Sudan has alternated between civilian and military rule, but a lasting solution to the country's political problems has eluded everyone who has tried to govern the nation.

The First Civilian Administration

Sudan, at independence, was set up as a democratic nation with three branches of government—the executive, the legislative, and the judicial branches. The nation's first prime minister was Isma'il al-Azhari, who had led the transitional government. However, Azhari's administration soon fell victim to political squabbling. Less than seven months after independence, on July 5, 1956, Azhari was replaced as prime minister by Abdallah Khalil.

Khalil set about addressing many of the problems facing Sudan, including the development of its educational system and the economy. Recognizing its unique dual heritage, the new government aligned itself not only with other African countries, but with countries in the Arab world, such as Syria and Saudi Arabia. However, continuing political infighting kept the government from accomplishing much, and in the face of increasing economic difficulties, the nation's military leaders lost patience. In a bloodless coup, General Ibrahim Abboud took over the governing of the country on November 17, 1958.

The Abboud Regime

General Ibrahim Abboud vowed to bring stability and what he called clean administration to the country. Abboud began by abolishing all political parties and creating a military council (called the Supreme Military Council) to rule Sudan. Like its civilian predecessor, the regime concentrated on improving the country's economic prospects and reducing political tensions. However, its handling of the simmering rebellion in the south brought the government much criticism. Abboud, believing that the problem of the south could be solved militarily, sent troops into southern Sudan to end all opposition to his regime. He also sought to integrate the south's educational system with the north's. He did this by expelling all Christian missionaries, who had operated most schools in the region. Having closed parliament and political parties, there was no forum in which complaints about Abboud's actions could be raised.

With no political outlet for their grievances, the southern leaders intensified the armed struggle against the government. Frustration over the escalating civil war in the south and economic setbacks culminated in a mass protest and strike by Sudanese professionals—for example, teachers and

These armed children formed part of a group of southern Sudanese insurgents that rebelled against General Ibrahim Abboud's rule in the early 1960s.

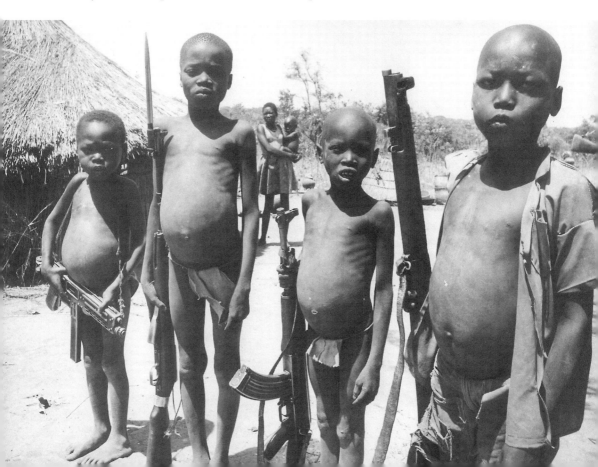

health care workers—in October 1964. The government's attempts to suppress the protests failed. As the protests intensified, Prime Minister Abboud resigned and dissolved the Supreme Military Council.

Following Abboud's resignation, a new transitional government headed by a civilian, Sirr al Khatim al Khalifa, assumed control of the country. However, the new civilian government lasted for barely a year, when it was overthrown by Colonel Gafaar Muhammed Nimeiri, ushering Sudan into its second military government and its fourth administration in less than ten years.

THE NIMEIRI REGIME

Following his coup, Nimeiri pronounced Sudan a socialist state. Much as the past military regime had done, Nimeiri prohibited all political parties and formed the ten-member

After failing to defeat the southern rebels, Sudanese leader Ibrahim Abboud (shown here with U.S. president John F. Kennedy) resigned in 1964.

Revolutionary Command Council to help him rule the country. The new leaders committed themselves to actions that would bring peace and stability to Sudan.

Despite general dissatisfaction with the former government's policies, there were many groups and individuals opposed to Nimeiri's rule. Muslims, especially, were concerned about the socialist policies of the new government. They felt that policies such as commercialization of banks and granting women equal rights conflicted with Islamic values. The internal conflicts created by Nimeiri's socialist views led to the first failed military coup against his government on July 19, 1971. Nimeiri would survive twenty-four other coups during his stay in office.

Heeding the demand to return the government to civilian rule, Nimeiri in 1972 called for elections in which he ran for the presidency and was subsequently elected. With his hold on power thus validated, Nimeiri determined to bring an end to the civil war, which he blamed for hampering Sudan's economic development. He met with rebel leaders in the Ethiopian capital, Addis Ababa, and hammered out an agreement that established the south as an autonomous political entity with its own regional assembly—High Executive Council or Cabinet—and a head of state who would also be the vice president of Sudan as a whole. The southern government would be responsible for all aspects of government in the region, except in such areas as defense, foreign affairs, currency and finance, economic and social planning, and interregional concerns. These functions remained under the jurisdiction of the national government. Southern representation in the national government was guaranteed, and amnesty was granted to southern rebels.

In the years following the Addis Ababa agreement, economic development projects were initiated in the south, and plans were made to explore and tap the oil reserves known to exist in the region. It seemed the south was well on its way to fulfilling its economic potential.

Having successfully tackled the southern problem, Nimeiri also sought reconciliation with the conservative Muslims who had been alienated by his government's initial socialist stance. Nimeiri's new policies tried to be mindful of the diverse cultural nature of Sudan. He renewed his commitment to a democratic system of government with equal representation for all Sudanese peoples. He tactfully addressed the religious question by promoting religious tolerance, recognizing Islam as the country's official religion but also recognizing that Christianity is the faith of a large number of Sudanese.

The initial success of the peace agreement in the south and the reconciliation with opposition leaders brought Nimeiri considerable international acclaim as a statesman. But problems soon returned. Internal squabbles, as well as allegations of corruption within the government, began to weaken Nimeiri's authority. In addition, the granting of autonomy to the south failed to prevent inequalities from arising in the way southern ethnic groups participated in the region's governance. For example, the formula for selecting members of the High Executive Council failed to keep the Dinka, who were the largest ethnic group in the south, from dominating the government. Under the leadership of the head of state Abel Alier, himself a Dinka, the Dinka quickly took for themselves positions of power and influence. Other ethnic groups objected to this monopolization of power, and internal conflict arose.

The other problem resulted from the question of how to use revenue acquired through the oil that would be exploited in the region. Many southerners believed that the oil proceeds should be used for their own economic development, but Nimeiri was adamant that the proceeds were to be used for the benefit of the whole country, north and south.

Faced with increasing unrest in the north resulting from the weakening of his authority, and the political conflicts in the south, Nimeiri adopted a more dictatorial style. He arrested and imprisoned without trial his political opponents. In an effort to weaken the Dinka hold on power in the south, Nimeiri suspended the Southern Regional Assembly and redivided the south into the three districts or provinces that had existed under colonial rule. Each province was granted its own ministers and assembly. The south opposed the redivision and called for a referendum on the situation. The request for a referendum was denied.

In order to shore up support for his crumbling regime among Sudan's Arab population, Nimeiri sought in 1983 to align his government with the teachings of Islam by introducing sharia, or Islamic law. Nimeiri further decreed that this policy would apply to the whole country, including the non-Islamic south. Sharia makes no distinction between religious and secular life, stipulating that both government as well as people's day-to-day lives should be conducted in accordance with the laws of Islam, which includes strict separation of men and women in all activities and severe penalties for those who break the laws, whether in private or public spheres.

While some traditionalists supported the imposition of sharia, there was strong opposition both domestically and internationally. Many political opponents were tried, imprisoned, or executed under the law for opposing the government's imposition of sharia. Others fled into exile.

After his efforts to introduce a democratic system of government failed, President Gafaar Muhammed Nimeiri adopted a dictatorial style based on strict observance of sharia, or Islamic law.

The southern response to Nimeiri's move was violent. Southern troops mutinied. A new militant organization, the Sudan People's Liberation Movement (SPLM), under Colonel John Guarang, its military leader, and Joseph Oduho, its political leader, began guerrilla attacks on government installations in the south. By the end of 1983, oil exploration in the south had stopped and the civil war was reignited, ravaging communities and destroying lives.

Dissatisfaction over the combination of the south's redivision, the introduction of sharia, the renewed civil war, and recurring economic problems eventually brought an end to Nimeiri's regime. In April 1985, while Nimeiri was on a visit to the United States, a group of military officers led by Lieutenant General Abdul Rahman Suwar Al-Dahab, deposed him. Nimeiri, on his way to Sudan, sought political asylum in Egypt.

SHARIA LAWS

Until 1983, the judicial system in Sudan was based on British laws, with special recognition of local customs. British laws were used to judge criminal and high-profile civil cases, while customary laws were applied to civil complaints, such as family and property disputes. However, in 1983, the Nimeiri government introduced sharia laws to be applied to every area of life—from criminal to minor civil cases. Sharia laws are based on Islamic beliefs and practices. Sharia promotes the strict separation of men and women in public and stipulates stiff punishment for anyone who breaks the custom. Punishment for stealing is amputation of the hand. Premarital pregnancy draws the penalty of death by stoning, as does adultery by either men or women. Even though the country still recognizes the civil courts, all Sudanese people, including non-Muslims, are bound to the Islamic legal system. This has been a source of intensified conflict, as non-Muslims believe that they should not be subject to the laws of a religion they do not practice. Non-Muslims would prefer a secular system rather than one ruled with the sharia.

TRANSITIONAL GOVERNMENT

Al-Dahab set up a transitional government that included many civilians. Within a year of his administration, Al-Dahab moved to return the country completely to civilian rule and called for general elections in which Saliq al-Mahdi was elected president. Al-Mahdi came from a prominent family, being the grandson of Muhammad al-Mahdi, who had led the rebellion against the Egyptians and the British during colonial times. Many people hoped that al-Mahdi would find a lasting solution to the country's political problems and restore stability to Sudan.

Al-Mahdi had been a strong opponent of Nimeiri's imposition of sharia, which he viewed as being incompatible with the realities of modern life. When he took office, al-Mahdi vowed to abolish sharia, but he found this difficult because of opposition from Islamic fundamentalists whose political support he needed. In an attempt at compromise, al-Mahdi tried eliminating the harshest aspects of sharia, such as penalties like amputation for stealing and stoning for adultery. He also introduced a policy that allowed the Muslim majority to choose the laws that would govern Muslims to the extent that these laws do not violate the rights of non-Muslims. On May 14, 1988, he created a twenty-seven-member government of national unity, in which northerners and southerners were to work toward national reconciliation.

Al-Mahdi's attempts to achieve a national consensus never got a chance to work, as economic and humanitarian crises engulfed Sudan. In August 1988, severe floods struck Sudan as the Nile's tributaries, swollen by rains, overflowed their banks. Ten thousand homes were swept away and close to a million people were displaced. In the south, where people were already starving because of the war, many thousands died because they were too weak to take care of themselves. Al-Mahdi was unable to overcome the economic and humanitarian disaster that ensued. Merely three years into his presidency, a military coup led by Lieutenant General Omar Hassan Ahmed al-Bashir ended the civilian government in April 1989.

BASHIR'S REGIME

General Bashir and his cohorts announced that the new regime had come to rescue the country from its political and economic problems and to bring stability. Bashir dissolved the civilian government and suspended the constitution. Many prominent politicians were arrested and detained, and all political parties, with the exception of Bashir's—the National Congress Party—were banned. A new body called the Revolutionary Command Council for National Salvation

---

 ## JOHN GUARANG

In the armed conflict between north and south, the political leader of the Southern People's Liberation Movement/Army (SPLM) is John Guarang. He was born in Jonglei in southern Sudan in 1943. From 1969 to 1970, he served in the Sudanese army, after which he worked as a lieutenant colonel at the Military Research Center in Khartoum. In May 1983, he founded the SPLM, which advocates for southern autonomy and greater participation of southern people in the economic and political processes in Sudan.

(RCC-NS), consisting of fifteen military officers under the leadership of the president, was installed to rule the country.

The challenges facing the new leaders, however, were identical to those faced by previous governments: what to do about sharia, what to do about the south, how to develop the country economically, and how to handle internal and external political conflicts. Many people hoped that the regime would rescind sharia. However, this did not happen, as most members of the RCC-NS were closely associated with the dominant Muslim group in the country, the fundamentalist National Islamic Front, which believed that there should be no separation of religion and state.

On January 20, 1991, instead of suspending sharia, the government renewed its commitment to running Sudan as an Islamic state. It declared that sharia should be enforced in the north and applied to all residents of the northern states, regardless of their religion. As during the Nimeiri era, people were required to live according to conservative Islamic principles. Men and women were prohibited from mingling in public and were required to sit in separate sections of public buses or other means of transportation. Women were required to wear clothing that completely covered their bodies, and they could not leave the country without the permission of a legal male guardian.

In keeping with Sudan being an Islamic state, all civil and criminal laws were made consistent with sharia. Arabic was made the only language of business and instruction in all public schools, including those in the south. Instead of Islam being taught as a subject in schools, as had been done in the past, the school curriculum was reformed to

President Saliq al-Mahdi tried to abolish sharia, but he met with stiff opposition from Islamic fundamentalists.

make Islamic principles and values part of all instruction. People who were considered not to be devout Muslims were fired from their jobs. The harsh penalties for violating sharia, such as amputation for stealing and stoning for adultery, were reimposed.

Al-Mahdi's government collapsed after failing to respond to the economic and humanitarian crises caused by the severe flooding of the Nile in August 1988.

A MOVE TOWARD OPENNESS

The international community, as well as many people in Sudan, voiced their concerns about the pro-Islamic stand of Bashir's government and condemned its strict social and political policies. In 1993, perhaps because of internal and external political pressure, the Bashir government initiated a series of democratic reforms. The RCC-NS was dissolved, and a transitional civilian government, with Bashir as prime minister, was installed. Three years later, general elections to select a formal civilian regime were held. Many opposition parties previously banned were allowed to participate in a show of the government's openness and tolerance of opposition. Bashir ran on his party's platform and was elected president.

Sharia dictates that women wear clothing that completely covers their bodies.

The validity of the election was open to question, however. For one thing, the south boycotted the elections in protest over the ongoing war the government was waging there. Moreover, many international observers said that the election was rigged, despite the government's claim to the contrary.

In any case, the new National Assembly, although meant to be representative of the country's diversity, was dominated by Bashir's party. Of the assembly's four hundred seats, 360 were held by the National Congress Party. Forty seats reserved for southern representatives remained vacant.

A New Constitution and a New Direction?

The dominance of members of the pro-Islamic National Congress Party assures that government policies remain pro-Islamic. The government argues that its Islamic orientation offers Sudan an advantage in that Islam provides an ethical framework for running the country that would otherwise be missing. "It is no shame to say that we are an Islamic government," said President Bashir in an interview. "It is an advantage to have an Islamic orientation. All governments would like to have an ethical standard, and religion provides the basis for ethics in government."[9]

A new constitution ratified in 1998, two years after the election, reinforced the identity of the country as an Islamic state, still maintaining sharia as the standard to be used for running both civil and criminal aspects of the society. The new constitution contains both dictatorial and democratic features. For example, it gives the president unlimited powers, including the power to assemble and dissolve the legislative branch of government. On the other hand, it provides for the reinstatement of political parties that were banned in 1989 and states that Sudan is committed to protecting individual human rights and openness to political debate.

In the years that followed, both democratic and undemocratic strands emerged. For example, in 1999, in response to political conflict, Bashir declared a state of emergency, dismissed the speaker of the National Assembly, and dissolved the legislature. Bashir's rationale was, ironically, that the speaker of the National Assembly, Dr. Turabi, was an obstacle to democratic changes and openness. Turabi was formerly an ally of the president, but had come to be seen as an impediment to reform. Of the rift with Turabi, Bashir indicated that

the split created an atmosphere conducive to the inclusion of various elements and political groups in society, whereas internationally it created an atmosphere that has enabled us to improve relations because Dr. Turabi was perceived as a major supporter of radical and Islamic groups.[10]

Another election was held in December 2000, and Bashir was reelected. This time, his National Congress Party won 355 of the 360 seats in the National Assembly. The forty seats slated for southern representatives remained vacant, as the south, now joined by many members of the opposition parties, boycotted the elections. Despite the lopsided results, some observers continue to argue that Bashir is committed to increasing political participation and inclusion of others in the political process.

Whatever the prospects for democracy in Sudan might be, the civil war that is ravaging lives and resources in the southern and western parts of the country remains the greatest concern for the people.

President Bashir was reelected in 2000, despite the fact that Sudan's long-running and bloody civil war continued to rage.

THE CIVIL WAR INTENSIFIES

Although many disagreements underlie the long-running civil war, one of the most intractable problems is the religious divisions within Sudan. The national government's insistence on adhering to sharia makes matters even worse. In fact, many secular Muslim groups opposed to the government's stand on sharia have joined the southern effort to fight Bashir's regime. The government indicates that while it is not willing to back away from its Islamic orientation, it is willing to seek a peaceful negotiation to the causes of the civil war.

Yet there are many other issues that are equally divisive. The government has met several times with representatives of the Southern Liberation Peoples' Movement/Army to iron out a cease-fire agreement. On the table, in addition to religious issues, are questions about the south's autonomy, the place of other groups not necessarily considered part of the south but whose lives have been affected tremendously by the war, security for the citizens, economic development, and equal distribution of resources in the country.

A COMPLEX POLITICAL SITUATION

As many people have pointed out, the conflict in Sudan is not only religious, it is ethnic and economic as well. Granting autonomy to the south in 1972, while it brought some degree of stability to the country, did not resolve all the conflicts. Actually, it brought to light the ethnic divisions within the south. The discovery of oil wells in the south during the 1970s only brought another bone of contention to the already difficult situation. The question, of course, became how much of the wealth derived from oil should be used by whom and for what purpose. The government would like to use all of the resources for the running of the country while southerners believe that it rightly belongs to them and should be used to develop their land. Furthermore, who should bear the expense of cleaning up the oil fields later on remains open.

Southern rebels like these are fighting to ensure southern Sudan enjoys greater political autonomy and receives an equitable share of the country's resources.

THE CIVIL WAR

In his book *Me Against My Brother*, journalist Scott Peterson laments the devastation brought on by the civil war in Sudan. He writes:

> Sudan's conflict today is a modern extension of the Crusades, of the collision between Islam and Christianity. As it was then, this war is still wholly primitive in its disregard for civilians. This is a battle in which there are no prisoners of war. And of course, these days it carries on with 20th-century weapons. Not every northern fighter is a bearded Muslim zealot swinging a sword for God's will. And not every southern rebel is a Christian soldier marching as to war. In fact, when the civil war first began more than 45 years ago, religion was hardly a factor. But, over time, religious aspects have turned into red lines. . . . Largely out of sight, Sudan's war has killed 1.5 million people—one out of every five southern Sudanese. That's more bodies than in Somalia and Bosnia combined; it's nearly double the toll of Rwanda's 1994 genocide.

In addition, while the north is Islamic, not all northerners are fundamentalist. The majority of the northern people opposes the government's fundamentalist stand and would prefer a secular government that understands and reflects the diverse cultures and peoples of Sudan. And while the south is predominately non-Islamic, 18 percent of its people are Islamic.

Most difficult of all problems is the one of trust. Even the government acknowledges that the southerners simply do not believe the promises northern leaders make. As a result, any agreement must be accompanied by measures that guarantee compliance by both sides with its terms, which is no easy task. Whether Sudan will float, or sink under its many problems, is still a question to be answered. Many are hopeful, indicating that peace and stability, as well as economic prosperity, is possible for Sudan. But they recognize that it will take the dedication of a highly gifted statesman who can make the right compromises that all Sudanese are willing to live with. Bashir thinks that he is that individual. The world is waiting to see.

THE CHALLENGES
OF EVERYDAY LIFE

Sudan's civil war, fueled by religious and ethnic differences, and its harsh climate combine to make life in Sudan difficult. Young people throughout the country find themselves conscripted to fight on one side or the other, and many lose their lives. In the south, where most of the fighting takes place, people struggle day to day just to survive. The topography of Sudan, with its deserts and rivers, while beautiful to the eye, renders the nation vulnerable to droughts and flooding. These natural hazards, intensified by the destruction caused by the war and the economic and social disruption that result, makes hunger a reality for many Sudanese.

"A LAND IN WAITING"

Sudan has the potential of being one of the richest countries in Africa. One writer describes it as "a land in waiting."[11] In the 1970s, during its brief period of peace, Sudan was even called a "breadbasket" of the Arab world. According to Robert O. Collins, many in the international community, especially the Arab countries, saw the economic and human potential of Sudan and were eager to help the country achieve that potential. "Arab oil producing states," he remarks, "as their own surpluses grew in the 1970s following increases in world petroleum prices, proposed in 1976 a program to develop Sudan as a breadbasket for the Arab world."[12] But when the war was reignited, much of the hope for economic prosperity died. As the twenty-first century opened Sudan, despite its potential, was one of the poorest countries in the world. The average household income was $139 a year. Many Sudanese were unemployed and, even when jobs were available, many lacked the skills needed to fill them.

The agricultural sector on which Sudan's economy depends employs 80 percent of the population. Abundant rainfall in the

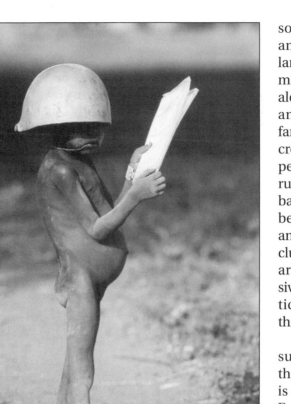

Many Sudanese children like this Dinka boy suffer from hunger and malnutrition.

south permits both farming and grazing ground for the large herds owned by the nomadic peoples. In the north, along the banks of the Nile and other rivers, irrigation farming prevails. Sudan's cash crops include cotton, sesame, peanuts, sugarcane, dates, citrus fruits, mangoes, coffee, tobacco, sorghum, millet, wheat, beans, cowpeas, pulses, corn, and barley. Other products include eucalyptus and gum arabic (used in various adhesives and in some pharmaceuticals) from the acacia that thrive in the region.

But even though Sudan supplies over 80 percent of the world's gum arabic, cotton is the principal export crop. Enough cotton is also produced by the nation's farmers to feed a sizable textile industry. In addition, Sudan is a major producer of meat and other livestock products, such as hides and skin. Among African nations, Sudan's livestock herd was second in size only to Ethiopia's in 1998. Oil found in the south still provides the country its greatest hope for economic survival.

LIFE IN THE CITIES

About 39 percent of Sudanese live in towns or cities, and these are located mostly in the northern part of Sudan. Not surprisingly, due to the dominance of Islam and the Arab culture in the north, life in the cities has an Arab-Islamic flavor, from the music heard on the streets to the clothes people wear. Cities and towns come to life every day at dawn as the faithful are called to their morning prayers. For a devout Muslim, this is the first of five daily prayers, recited while kneeling, prostrate, and facing east, the direction of the Muslim holy city of Mecca.

Daily life in the city is vibrant but predictable. People either walk to their jobs or use the always available taxis and buses. Only those who can afford it—and many cannot—have their own cars. Business hours are from 8:00 A.M. to 2:00 P.M. and from 6:00 P.M. to 8:00 P.M., Saturday through Thursday, with Friday as the day of rest. Because the temperature is hottest from 2:00 P.M. to 6:00 P.M., people often stay indoors visiting with friends or taking siesta. Christians are legally allowed two hours on Sundays to attend church services if they wish.

After work, Sudanese city dwellers relax with their families. As one writer states, "spending time together is a vital part of Arab community living, and for one to deny his friends or family of this time is highly looked down upon."[13] Some—mostly men—sometimes join friends to socialize at one or another of the few restaurants around town. Due to Sudan's

A man dries cattle hides. Sudan remains one of Africa's leading producers of livestock products like meat and hides.

strict application of sharia, alcoholic drinks are not served, and gambling is forbidden. There are also a few entertainment opportunities, like open-air theaters, which feature native dances and movies, mostly in Arabic. The content of public shows and films is monitored and censored by the appropriate government agency to ensure compliance with Islamic moral standards. However, many Sudanese, unless business or other duties dictate, prefer staying home in the evenings and listening to the radio or watching state-sponsored programs on television.

LIFE IN THE COUNTRYSIDE

Although Sudan is seeing increasing numbers of people leaving rural areas to search for a higher standard of living in the cities, the majority of people, roughly 60 percent, still live in the country, usually in small villages. Most people in rural areas are farmers or cattle herders—some combine the two. Everybody in the family, from the young to the aged, has specific assigned duties for the maintenance of the family and the entire community.

In rural Sudan, most people live close to other members of their extended family. Since both Islam and indigenous African religions allow more than one wife, extended families can be quite large. In polygamous households, each wife has her own house within the large family compound, which she shares with her young children. A boy leaves his mother's house, usually after his circumcision or initiation ceremony,

 SUDANESE CITIES

Sudanese cities are home to politicians, merchants, students, and public servants involved in all areas of life as teachers, doctors, nurses, etc. Cities are also home to those employed in the many industries and business centers. They are home, also, to the many unemployed or grossly underemployed citizens who moved to the cities looking for a better way of life only to be disappointed by the lack of opportunities. Like in many cities around the world, living conditions vary from the highly modern and well-furnished houses of the rich and elite to the slums where the newly arrived and refugees from the war in the south and other parts of Africa live.

and either builds his own house within the compound or shares one with other boys his age.

Houses are made of mud with thatched roofs. The shape varies from round to rectangular based on preference. Beginning in the 1980s, however, cement-brick houses with metal roofs became common. Most houses lack electricity and indoor plumbing. Light is obtained from open fires, candles, or kerosene lamps. Water is obtained from the nearby streams, rivers, or wells. Family meals are prepared over open fires. Because of the relatively small number of people living in each village, life is close-knit and people know each other and collectively help and support their fellow residents.

The routine of daily life in the countryside rarely varies. Usually the village wakes up at dawn. People scatter to perform their early morning tasks, including fetching water, milking the animals, and cleaning the compound area. As in the cities, Muslims say their morning prayers. Depending on their traditions, non-Muslims may or may not engage in some religious observance. A light breakfast—consisting of milk (with or without tea) and bread, or sometimes corn porridge—is eaten, and soon people are off to their daily tasks. Those children who have been enrolled in school find their way to their classes; those who are not in school begin their assigned tasks, which for girls is helping around the house and caring for the younger children. Boys perform such light farm duties as bird scaring, to keep birds from eating farm crops, and looking after goats and other domestic stock near the home. Men and older boys take the cattle out to pasture.

As night falls, people return home. The cattle are milked and secured for the night. The evening meal, which often consists of milk, rice and vegetables, or stewed beans (ful), is prepared and eaten. After the evening meal, it is time to play, tell stories, and relax. "If the weather persists," says Janice Boddy, "neighbors sit talking beneath the stars until their babies drop off to sleep."[14] Celebration of special occasions and village gatherings occur in the evenings as well.

Among the nomadic and seminomadic Sudanese, daily life is dependent on the climate. Nomadic families are always on the move, looking for good pasture for their cattle. Even in the more settled communities, however, except

Rural Sudanese live as close-knit families in towns like this one comprised of small huts with thatched roofs.

where irrigation allows for better yields, most people manage to grow only enough food for their own use. If the rain fails, as it often does, or if there is severe flooding, the harvest is lost and the people struggle to survive. Also affecting the lives of those living in rural areas is lack of accessibility to major markets for the sale of their products. The villagers, lacking such access, instead sell their goods to area wholesale merchants who pay as little as possible for goods. Often there is only one such merchant in an area. The absence of competition gives the merchant an advantage over the villagers, who have little leverage in bargaining.

In the war-ravaged south, life is even more difficult, as many people have to move quickly to avoid being caught in the crossfire between the warring factions. "School children, for example, listen to the teacher with one ear and listen for the sound of military airplanes with the other,"[15] notes one news report from Sudan. Many parents, fearing for the lives of their children, have taken them out of school completely,

since the location of schools in open spaces, and the con-
centration of so many people in one place, make them
tempting targets for air strikes.

FAMILY LIFE

Whether living in the city or the country, the family unit is
important in Sudan, and most Sudanese are expected to
marry and become parents. For females especially, marriage
is significant because, in most communities, a girl, regardless
of age, is not considered an adult until she marries. In addition, marriage is viewed as a union between two families
rather than just between the bride and the groom. Thus,
even though increasing numbers of Sudanese freely choose
their own spouses, the custom of arranged marriages still
prevails. A man pays dowry in the form of money or cattle to
his bride's family at marriage.

In Sudan, divorce is legal, although in most communities
it is discouraged. If a divorce does occur, the wife's family is
expected to return the dowry as long as no child has been
born to the marriage. However, if the woman has borne

 ## BRIDE WEALTH

Sudanese men pay bride wealth, or dowry, for
their wives. The dowry is a gift given to the bride or the bride's
family by the groom. Among some ethnic groups such as
Dinka, Baggara, and Nuer, the dowry is in the form of cattle.
An agreement is reached between the groom and the bride's
parents as to the number of cattle to be given. When the cattle
are received, the bride's family distribute the cattle among
their relatives. Also, in some communities, the bridegroom
has to perform work for his prospective father-in-law. In farming communities, such as among the Nuba, this service takes
the form of several days' work tilling the ground or doing
other necessary tasks. A marriage is not considered legal until
the dowry has been received in full. The dowry, however, does
not represent payment for the bride. It is rather viewed as
compensation to the bride's family for the loss of a working
member and considered a token of respect for the bride and
her family. In return for the dowry, the bride's family sends
their daughter to her new home with most of the items she
would need to set up house.

children, the bride's family keeps the dowry as compensation for the children, who remain part of the husband's family. Children who are very young when their parents divorce live with their mothers. But once a male child can take care of his own physical needs, usually between age six and ten, he is expected to go back to his father's family compound.

EDUCATION

Even though Sudanese place a high value on their children, they struggle to make their educational system meet the needs of their growing population. The country's literacy rate stands at 43 percent; the fact that the literacy rate for those thirty-five and older stands at 75 percent suggests how dysfunctional the nation's schools have become.

The government has worked to improve the educational system, but the weak economy makes for limited financial resources. Sudanese who are well off and live in the cities can receive a good education in private schools. The majority of Sudanese, however, live in rural areas where government and private schools both suffer from lack of funds. Teachers are often poorly qualified; many primary school teachers, for example, hold only a high school diploma. The teachers are also poorly paid; every year, Sudan loses many qualified teachers to other Arab nations where the pay is better. In some rural areas, there is no government-provided educational facility. The local people, through self-help initiatives, build makeshift schools and hire teachers to staff them. In the war-torn areas of the south, there is minimal opportunity to go to school at all.

THE SCHOOL SYSTEM

The school year runs from July to March, with a three-month break from April to June. The school year also observes a number of public and religious holidays, such as Independence Day, New Year's Day, al-Fitr—the feast that celebrates the end of the fasting month, or Ramadan—and al-Adha—the feast that follows the pilgrimage to Mecca.

The school system has an eight-three structure: eight years of basic schooling, the equivalent of American primary and intermediate levels, and three years of high school or technical/vocational school. Instruction is in Arabic, although English is offered as a foreign language in grades seven through eleven.

Basic education is compulsory, even though the policy is not strictly enforced. Most Sudanese children, especially in rural areas, drop out after six years so that they can help around the house, in the fields, or with herding animals. Nomad children are especially likely to lack schooling, since their families are always on the move and parents tend not to see the value of a formal education.

At the end of every school year, students must pass the year's exam in order to move on to the next grade. Basic education students must also pass the Basic Education Certificate Examination in order to move on to high school. High school students must pass the School Certificate Examination to qualify for admission into a university or some other institution of higher learning. Some high school students who fail this exam find employment teaching primary school while studying for and retaking the exams to qualify for further studies. The vocational schools offer training in agriculture, industry, and commerce for boys, and home economics

Poor schoolchildren draw on the ground during a lesson. Although basic education is compulsory, most Sudanese children leave school at a young age to work on the family farm.

for girls. Vocational students also must pass their own version of the School Certificate Examination at the end of their study.

KORANIC SCHOOLS

Even though the curriculum in most schools, especially in the north, is in line with Islamic principles, many Sudanese children attend Koranic schools, where they learn the basic tenets of Islam. Both boys and girls attend Koranic schools, although girls are expected to drop out once they reach puberty. Adult males who want to increase their knowledge of Islam may also attend Koranic schools. Koranic schools might consist of a building put up for that purpose, or students may meet in the mosque or the teacher's home. School is held every night except Thursday, when people prepare for the Muslim sabbath the following day.

At the Koranic schools, the pupils sit on the floor, their legs crossed, facing the Imam (religious teacher). Their eyes are attentive as they memorize, recite, and copy passages from the Koran. Some students will spend just a few years in the Koranic school, while others will spend significant portions of their lives learning about their religion and the Islamic way of life. Upon graduating, students who want may further their knowledge of Islam by attending Islamic high schools, according to information from the Sudanese Embassy in London. And those who are further interested in pursuing Arabic and Islamic studies and have the means to do so can attend one of two universities in Sudan—Omdurman Islamic University or University of Holy Quran and Islamic Sciences—which are dedicated to Islamic religious studies.

HIGHER EDUCATION

For those students who score well on the School Certificate Examination, university is an option. Sudan has several institutions of higher learning, including the University of Khartoum, Khartoum Polytechnic, with branches all over the country, El-Nilein University (formerly Cairo University, Khartoum Branch), Omdurman Islamic University, University of Holy Quran and Islamic Sciences, University of Juba, University of Gezira, and higher technical and teacher-training colleges. Students can obtain full or partial scholarships to attend these institutions.

The University of Khartoum, however, with a total under-graduate student population of 16,800 and 6,000 graduate students, is the country's premier institution of higher learning and its center of intellectual life. It accepts only top students from the country's high schools. The government pays all cost for attending the university, which makes it the top choice for aspiring high school students. The university awards degrees in the sciences, arts and humanities, social sciences, law, medicine, and various other disciplines. The course of study lasts from four to six years, depending on the field of study.

Prior to 1983, instruction in the University of Khartoum and most other institutions of higher learning was conducted in English. However, when Sudan was pronounced an Islamic country in 1983, the language of instruction was changed to Arabic. English, though, is taught as a foreign language, and most Sudanese college graduates can speak both English and Arabic.

All institutions of higher learning have separate facilities and centers for their female students, in keeping with the

Sudanese students who receive a high score on the high school exit exam can attend one of the country's many universities.

Islamic code of separation of men and women in public. There is also a private university for women, Ahfad University College for Women, in Omdurman. The institution is dedicated to preparing women for both academic and public life, offering programs in child care, women's health, and leadership training. Some of its graduates work for nonprofit organizations in rural areas where they teach other women basic skills, such as reading, caring for their families, treating minor aliments, and managing their own finances.

HEALTH

Many Sudanese, like this tuberculosis patient, suffer from serious illnesses like malaria, dysentery, and typhoid.

Sudan's entire education system has been greatly weakened by the economic consequences of frequent droughts, flooding, and civil conflicts. These same factors burden Sudanese health facilities, which in any case have always been inadequate. There is a high rate of infant and maternal mortality, especially in rural areas, and overall the average life expectancy in Sudan is fifty-six years. Hunger and malnutrition make children and adults susceptible to various diseases, including malaria, typhoid, dysentery, and other intestinal aliments. Tuberculosis and blindness are common in the north, and sleeping sickness, which is spread by tsetse flies, is a serious problem in the south.

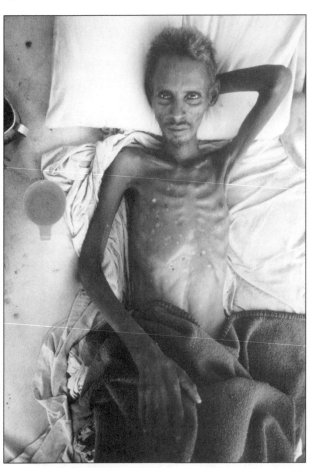

Sudan does have private and public hospitals and clinics. It also has well-trained doctors, nurses, and public health workers. But the hospitals are mostly in the cities, and about half of the health care professionals live in the cities. This means that people in the countryside must fend for themselves, often relying on folk remedies that are of

SLAVERY IN SUDAN

Thousands of women and children, primarily in the south, are kidnapped every year from their homes and villages and taken to other parts of the country, and perhaps the world, where they are used in forced labor. According to a report in a website sponsored by the *Washington Times*, www.internationalreports.net, some argue that "the allegations of slavery are little more than a misrepresentation of a centuries-old practice of child abductions, usually by rival tribes, to increase the number of workers needed for herding and other agricultural activities." The United Nations International Children's Emergency Fund (UNICEF) and Save the Children give the number of abducted women and children at 14,000, while other organizations put it higher—at 40,000 to 50,000. The Sudanese government, which had denied charges pertaining to this practice for a long time, is now acknowledging that it is a problem that ought to be tackled and stopped. In 2003, more than a million dollars were donated by various international agencies to fund organizations in Sudan working to end child abductions and other human rights issues. About 2,000 abducted children have been documented and photographed, and, of these, 350 have been returned to their families. The rest, who were abducted at such a young age that they do not know how to get home, are kept in a network of peace-building centers that are run by UNICEF and Save the Children. There, these youngsters are provided with food, shelter, and schooling.

limited effectiveness. The weak economy limits the availability of medicines and other medical equipment, even in the cities. The wealthy few, of course, can receive adequate medical care by going abroad for treatment. The majority of Sudanese, however, must cope the best they can.

The government has promised to spend money in combating illness and updating the nation's health care system. But all is dependent on achieving political and economic stability and obtaining revenue from oil reserves that are still largely untapped.

FOR WOMEN, A DAILY STRUGGLE

The challenges of daily life in Sudan fall most heavily on the nation's women. As the primary caregivers and homemakers

Life in Sudan is difficult for the nation's women. In addition to bearing responsibility for most domestic chores, women face discrimination in most areas of Sudanese society.

for their families, they carry the responsibility for looking after members of both the immediate and extended family. They take care of the young, the old, and the sick, a job made all the more difficult by the limited economic and health resources available in the country. In the south, the responsibility is intensified by the uncertainty and destruction brought on by war.

Culture and long-standing custom impose their own limitations on women. In conservative Arab communities, for instance, women's lives are limited to the homes. "Except for a small number of liberated, educated young women from families of the elite, women remained within the household and were segregated at all festivities, eating after the men," according to Collins. Even when she is fortunate enough to receive an education and be employed outside the home, "she is not exempt from the traditional restrictions and supremacy of the Muslim husband. She is aware that her education and job is not a license to trespass upon male-dominated social norms,"[16] he maintains.

However, restrictions on women's lives are not limited only to Arab communities. Even in the south or among the Baggara nomads, where women are actively involved in the social and economic life of their communities, women are still forbidden by law to own land or cattle, the two most essential forms of wealth in these cultures. Such customs perpetuate poverty and female dependency on men.

Moreover, in 1983, when Sudan's government implemented a strict enforcement of sharia, the political situation of many women further deteriorated. Many women who were employed in the civil service lost their jobs because sharia forbids the employment of women outside the home, especially in places where they may come in contact with men. Educational opportunities were further curtailed as women were removed from regular classrooms and placed in all-female classes where the quality of instruction was substandard. Women were no longer free to travel abroad without the permission of a male family member. Those who went out in public with an uncovered head or who wore slacks, perceived as a sign of rebelliousness, were arrested. In 1991, for example, twenty-five female university students in Khartoum were sentenced to be flogged simply for wearing trousers instead of the garb dictated by Islam.

More recently, some restrictions on women have eased. The 1998 constitution returned some of the rights women lost in 1983. The constitution guarantees gender equality and the right of women to economic and political freedom. Women have the right to vote and to receive equal education. Twenty-seven seats in the National Assembly are reserved for women. In addition, a number of women's organizations in the country are working on behalf of women and their interests. For example, some are working to ban the practice of female circumcision, which is widespread in northern Sudan.

Still, a lack of access to education remains a problem for women; roughly 70 percent of Sudanese women cannot read and write. It will be a long time before women are considered equal partners with men in deciding social, economic, and political issues in Sudan.

The challenges of living in a harsh climate, deepened by the devastation of a protracted civil war, are immense.

FEMALE RITUALS

In his essay on the lives of Sudanese women, which appears in *Sudan: A Country Study*, Robert O. Collins indicates that female circumcision and the Zar cult are two traditional customs that hold enormous private and social significance. He states:

> Zar was the name given to the ceremony conducted only by women practitioners required to pacify evil spirits and to cleanse women of afflictions caused by demons or jinn. Zar cults were numerous throughout Muslim Africa. Illnesses, including depression, infertility, and other organic and psychological disorders, were attributed to possession by hostile spirits. Although Zar ceremonies varied widely, they not only freed the one possessed, but were great social occasions where women could communicate together as men did within male circles.

> Female circumcision was widely practiced throughout Muslim Africa, especially among Sudan's northern Arab population. Enormous pressure was put on the twelve-year-old or younger girl, as well as older women and their families, to observe these rituals and practices.

Whether living in the city or the countryside, Sudanese in general face great economic and social challenges. The country is blessed with great natural resources which, if developed to their potential, can help the nation's leaders alleviate suffering, improve educational opportunities, and provide basic social services. But first, the country needs to arrive at a peaceful settlement for its political problems.

Arts and Culture

Sudan boasts a rich cultural heritage that is reflected in its arts and literature, as well as in other aspects of life—from food to clothing to festivals. Despite its struggling economy and the disruptions brought by the civil war, the people find ways to preserve their diverse artistic and cultural heritage.

Ancient Relics

One way Sudanese seek to celebrate their culture is by preserving relics of Sudan's ancient civilizations. Such relics include grand and intricate architectural works, statues, and monuments commemorating the kings and queens who once ruled the land. The ancient Cush and Nubian civilizations (3500 B.C.–A.D. 350) and the civilizations that developed following the introduction of Christianity and Islam during A.D. 600 and 700, created in Sudan architectural wonders that amaze modern archaeologists. Some of the relics of these past civilizations include large palace complexes built of brick and containing elaborate swimming pools and temples built for local gods, as well as grand cathedrals and mosques.

Between the Blue Nile and the Atbara, where historians place the ancient city of Meroe—the later capital of Cush—archaeologists have uncovered ruins of the residence of the candances, the Cush rulers. The ruined structures attest to the rich lifestyle of their former inhabitants. The palace includes shops on the lower levels, large rooms where affairs of state were conducted, and richly decorated temples. The design of these structures reflects ancient Sudan's historical contact with other ancient cultures, including Egypt, India, China, and Rome.

Archaeologists, recognizing the cultural significance of Sudan's ancient relics, are feverishly excavating known sites and searching for others whose existence is suspected but not confirmed. One particularly significant find was that by a group of archaeologists from Switzerland's University of Geneva, who discovered a pit filled with large monuments and finely carved statues of Nubian kings. The statues are highly polished, finely carved, and made of granite, with the name of the king engraved on the back and feet of each sculpture. "The statues are sculptural masterpieces and important additions to our knowledge of the history of the region,"[17] said Charles Bonnet, an archaeologist who led the team.

The Sudanese government indicates that there are thousands of such sites yet to be fully excavated. When they are, the finds promise to add to the already existing magnificent collections that attest to the wealth and rich culture of Sudan's antiquity.

To preserve them from thieves, the smaller, more easily moved antiquities have been relocated to several museums around Sudan, including the National Museum in Khartoum. In addition to these museums, some private houses and palaces of historical significance are also used to house artifacts from more recent history. One such place is the

Sudan's many archaeological relics, like the ruins of this Roman temple in Naqa, reflect the grandeur of the country's ancient civilizations.

house of Imam Al-Mahdi's successor, the Khalifa, who led the Sudanese in their revolution against the Egyptians and the British (1882–1899).

Modern-day Sudanese artists continue to celebrate their heritage in their intricate designs of buildings, both religious and secular, through the inclusion of important religious motifs. In the south, for instance, Shilluk paint pictures of crocodiles and ostriches onto the walls of shrines dedicated to Nyikang, their mythical ancestor. The crocodile is an important symbol in the Shilluk religion. In folk mythology, Nyikang's mother is said to have been a crocodile, or part crocodile. Shilluk make offerings at riverbanks to this matriarch.

Sudan's cultural heritage comes through also in arts and crafts, including wood carving; basket weaving; and pottery, jewelry, and leather making. The objects that craftspeople make are for household use, as well as for sale in the markets, where they are purchased for their aesthetic qualities.

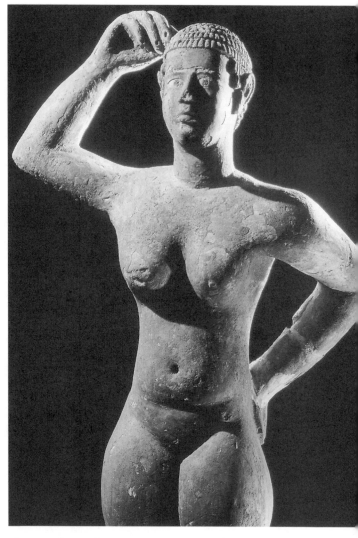

A number of beautiful small antiquities, like this Cushite statue from Meroe, are housed in Khartoum's National Museum.

WOOD CARVING

Sudanese wood-carvers make everything from small household goods, such as wooden spoons and bowls, to large items, such as elaborately decorated tables and beds. To some Sudanese, wood carving is a livelihood; to others, it is a hobby, a reminder of the old days when wood carving was a communal activity engaged in by men between planting and harvesting seasons. In the past, Azande were renowned for such wood carving and created sculptures that were probably given as gifts to chiefs; such items were purely works of art. Some such artworks were functional, such as boxes used to store honey and other goods; others possessed spiritual significance, such as the Yanda figures, spiritual effigies used in Azande religious ceremonies.

Today, as in the past, Azande are also famous for making elaborately decorated but powerful knives and daggers with carved wooden handles. There is the *shongo*, a multibladed throwing knife that spins as it flies, making it an extremely dangerous weapon in the hands of an expert. There is also

For centuries, craftsmen like this goldsmith have produced intricate and beautiful wares in Sudan.

the sickle-shaped knife that is as lethal as the *shongo*. These daggers are highly valued by Azande, and often function as money, particularly for bride-wealth gifts, which compensate a woman's family for the loss of her labor when she marries and moves to her husband's home.

Dinka and Shilluk also make an art of wood carving, producing elaborate wooden headrests. In the past, the headrests served in place of pillows and were particularly useful in keeping elaborate hairstyles from being ruined during sleep. Today, these headrests are more likely to be pressed into service as low stools and used when elderly visitors show up, since it is considered inappropriate for the elderly to have to sit on the floor.

POTTERY

While wood carving is mostly perceived a as a craft practiced by men, pottery is usually created by women. Clay items such as pots and bowls are vital for cooking and carrying water, which are traditional women's activities, so making these objects falls to them as well. For the most part, in Sudan, pottery making is seen as mundane, although it takes practice to make a good pot. Coils of clay are molded by hand into the desired shape. Then the edges are moistened and smoothed down. Color is added by rubbing with a colored stone, and patterns are inscribed using a sharp tool. The pot is then fired by placing it overnight in a hole in the ground and covering it with burning straw and dung. Designs on the pots vary among Sudan's different peoples. Some pots have flower designs; others carry geometric symbols. The designs may be simply decorative or convey some deeper symbolism.

LEATHER WORKING

Just like wood carving and pottery, leather working has long been practiced in Sudan. Because most Sudanese raise cattle and other types of hide-producing animals, leather working thrives in Sudan. Leather items such as blankets, bags, purses, and sandals are found in most Sudanese homes.

Products made from leather are strong and resist wear, so they are practical as well as aesthetically pleasing. The artists decorate their products to suit their taste and imagination, and to appeal to potential buyers if the article is for sale. Baggara women, for instance, elaborately decorate the leather blankets they use to adorn their camels. These blankets are decorated with cowrie shells and various artistic patterns according to the taste and means of the artist.

THE ORAL TRADITION

Similar to its visual arts and ancient and modern architecture, Sudan has a rich and extensive literary heritage that reflects the diverse cultures of its people. Modern Sudanese literature combines both written and oral literary traditions. Storytelling, proverbs, songs, poetry, and music form an integral part of life as people use these expressive forms as means of preserving and transferring community values.

As in many African countries, oral literature, which includes myths, legends, folktales, proverbs, and poetry, serves important community functions for Sudanese. The stories and recitations are used for entertainment and for teaching the young valuable life lessons. Every ethnic group in Sudan has its own cherished tales of the deeds of its ancestors, tales that celebrate survival skills and remind the people of their collective identity.

The telling of stories is woven into the fabric of daily life. At the end of the day, when chores are done, children and adults relax and enjoy each other's company by telling stories. At important family occasions, when an elder wants to stress a point without being too direct, the individual would almost always tell a folktale. The message is never lost; the intricacies of the stories are never forgotten.

MODERN WRITERS

Educated Sudanese are preserving some of their oral traditions by writing some of the works down. They are also creating new stories based on their own experiences. Sudan is home to well-known as well as emerging writers who produce novels, short stories, and poetry that build upon the old to reflect their interpretation of modern life. They celebrate or critique their cultural and social heritage while expressing their hope for the future of their country.

The best known Sudanese writer, and the first to gain international renown, is Al-Tayeb Salih. He is the author of many short stories and several novels, including *The Wedding of Zein, Seasons of Migration to the North*—his best-known work—and *Bandarshah*, as of 2003 his most recent

work. Other writers include the controversial woman writer, Kola Boof (born Naima Alu Kolbookek), and poets Taban Lo Liyong, Akol Meyan Kuol, and Leila Aboulela.

MUSIC

Just as crafts and literature do, music serves both practical and artistic purposes. Sudanese music ranges from the Arab-influenced songs of the north to the more traditional African-sounding songs and chants of the south. Some songs are associated with religious festivals and ceremonies and are sung accompanied by instruments and dancing. Others, such as the cattle songs of the Baggara and Dinka, tell about the demands as well as the beauty of the nomadic way of life. However, no matter what their theme or message, songs bring joy to the people and reinforce their cultural identity and heritage.

Often, too, music is used to express feelings about contemporary events. Songs have been used by various Sudanese political factions to encourage and incite followers to action; they have also been used to mourn a passing way of

The cattle songs of the Dinka and Baggara celebrate the freedom of the nomadic way of life. Sudan's many ethnic groups use such songs to reinforce their unique cultural identities.

Sudanese men in ceremonial dress perform a wedding dance. Dance forms and rituals vary among Sudan's many ethnic groups.

life. For instance, most songs that came from Nubia in the 1960s mourned the loss of their homeland, which was flooded by the building of the Aswan High Dam in Egypt. Even songs being composed almost forty years later remind the people of this sad time in their history.

Drums are a major musical instrument and are often accompanied by the lyre, which goes under a number of different names such as tambour among the Nubians and *brimbiri* among the Nuba. Most Sudanese lyres have metal strings. Harps, one-stringed fiddles, flutes, trumpets, and horns are also popular. Most music is accompanied by dancing and clapping.

Dance forms vary among the ethnic groups. For instance, the Nuba have a dance called the *kambala*, performed during rain or harvest ceremonies. The dancers wear horns of huge bulls on their heads as a sign of power. They also adorn themselves with bells and anklets to give stronger sounds during the dance. The Dinka are known for their "leaping dance." As its name suggests, the dance is performed by dancers leaping with the drum beats. Then there is the sword dance, favored by the ethnic groups in eastern Sudan. During the dance, men and women stand in two opposing lines, with the men carrying their swords as a symbol of courage and chivalry.

DRESS

As in art, literature, and music, the types of clothing worn in Sudan also reflect the country's cultural diversity as well as practical needs. In the north, men and women wear clothes that cover their entire bodies, as dictated by their Islamic faith. In the south, where the influence of Islam is slight, people wear less clothing in deference to the hot, humid weather.

Much of Sudanese traditional dress is elaborate. Baggara women, for instance, wear heavy jewelry of gold and silver.

Baggara men wearing long white robes and head wraps make their way to worship at their village mosque.

The more elaborate the working on the jewelry, the more prosperous the woman and the more social prestige is given her. The clothes of Baggara men, although less elaborate than the women, are nonetheless distinctive. They wear the traditional long, white gown and shave their heads in defense against insects and then wrap their heads with white cloth. Among the Dinka, both men and women, especially unmarried individuals, wear beaded clothing. Unmarried women wear bodices made up of thousands of tiny, colored beads. These hang from the neck like very wide necklaces. Dinka men may also wear a similar garment, a kind of beaded corset. Such beaded clothing, how-

A DYING ART

One of the striking ancient arts of Sudan is body scarring and decoration. Each ethnic group distinguishes itself from the others through distinctive body scarring patterns. The scarring also symbolizes individual milestones or acceptance of the people's way of life. The patterns used to decorate the skin are rich in community as well as personal symbolism.

The Nuba, Nuer, Shilluk, and Dinka are famous for their elaborate body scarring and painting. The scarring process is arduous and requires courage. The skin is cut in patterns and then rubbed with ash, saliva, or sesame oil, to help darken the scars and promote healing. The time for scarring differs among ethnic groups. For the Nuba, the first scarring is done in childhood or at the start of puberty and may continue for years. For women, the final scarring takes place after they have weaned their first child. The scars fade with age and become less prominent. Among the Nuer, Dinka, and Shilluk, the first scarring is done during a person's initiation ceremony; the others are received as the individual matures and crosses specific milestones, such as marriage, birth of the first child, etc.

Body painting is less painful than scarring and is done more frequently. The style, pattern, and design depend on the taste of the wearer and are influenced by current fashions, which change every few years. However, as these ethnic groups are otherwise occupied by the civil war, body painting and scarring are in danger of falling into disuse.

ever, is not very practical and so is largely reserved for ceremonial occasions.

Food

Just as clothing varies from one particular ethnic group to another, so too does food vary. Sudan's staple food, however, eaten by peoples of various ethnic groups, is *ful*, made from cooked beans and served with raw onions or mixed vegetables. However, the differences in lifestyle as well as climate often account for differences among the various ethnic groups in the foods they eat. Nomads, for instance, rely on milk and other dairy products for food, since these are produced by their animals wherever they happen to be. Southern farmers eat more vegetables because the climate is favorable for growing them and the people generally plan on being around to harvest them. Whether nomads or settled farmers, Sudanese tend not to eat beef, since killing cattle for meat is considered a waste of valuable resources. Goat and chicken, therefore, are preferable as sources of protein. But when a cow dies, as a result of old age or an accident, the meat is eaten.

The Koran forbids the eating of pork and shellfish, as such food is considered unclean. But some ethnic groups such as the Nuba—who before the coming of Islam relished pork—still eat it in spite of the dictates of the religion. The Sudanese diet, as in many African countries, is supplemented by fruit, nuts, and roots that grow in abundance in the region.

Festivals

As a result of their rich culture and history, Sudanese people often find many occasions to celebrate life and their diverse cultural heritage. They observe a mixture of Muslim and other religious festivals, as well as secular holidays, such as New Year's Day, Independence Day, and Unity Day. In the non-Muslim communities of the south, the time between the harvest and the dry seasons is the occasion for many social events, including engagements, marriages, and initiation ceremonies. There are also events, such as birth and naming ceremonies, that take place year-round. During these celebrations, communities come together to renew their interconnection as a unique people. Such occasions are also opportunities for much eating, dancing, and singing.

Sudan also observes Muslim holidays, ceremonies, and festivals. These include the seven major Islamic celebrations: al-fitr—the feast that celebrates the end of the fasting month, or Ramadan; al-Adha—the feast that follows the pilgrimage to Mecca; Lilat-al-Qadar—celebrating the night of the first revelation of the Koranic verses to Muhammad; Isra'Wal Mirag—commemorating the night that the prophet Mohammed is said to have flown to Jerusalem and from there to the seventh sky to establish the Five Pillars of the Islamic faith; al Sana al-Higriah—the Islamic New Year; and Mulid-al-Nabi—the prophet Muhammad's birthday. Easter and Christmas are observed by the few Christians in the nations, although these holidays usually are celebrated on a more modest scale than Islamic and other festivals.

A VIBRANT CULTURE

From the varieties of festivals and food to literature and visual arts, both modern and ancient, Sudan is home to a vibrant culture that reflects the people's love of life and their complex, rich, and diverse histories. Sudan's historical back-

Conflicts between Sudan's many ethnic groups like these Arabic nomads have resulted in a prolonged civil war. Sudan's future depends on resolution of the country's political crises.

BETTER OFF BECAUSE OF THE WAR

In an interview he granted in 2001, a former civilian prime minister of Sudan, Sadiq al-Mahdi, gives an optimistic evaluation of current social and political situation in Sudan. He argues that Sudan is in many ways ahead of its neighbors in dealing with the thorny issue of bridging its traditional past with the modern world. He says that in most other countries in the region, the types of cultural conflicts based on ethnic and religious divisions that have resulted in civil war and great suffering in Sudan have been swept under the rug by authoritarian governments. In Sudan, the problems are on the surface and are being dealt with, one way or the other. As they are solved, Sudan will gain strength and grow as a state that has institutions that accommodate its diversity. He believes that even though Sudan may look a lot worse than many of its neighbors, it is in fact the healthiest because it is dealing with its problems and will be healed of them as a result.

ground, its geographical distributions, and its rich cultural diversity combine to give the country a unique position in Africa. Sudanese consider their country the richest nation in Africa in terms of history and cultural heritage.

But this same heritage is the cause of the conflict that has plunged Sudan into the prolonged civil war that has damaged its economy and its people's sense of well-being. Sudanese recognize the unique opportunities their country is missing because of the civil war. They recognize the great cultural potential with which they have been endowed and the need for peace. Government representatives and the southern rebels continue to hold meetings in order to negotiate peace. Some peace talks have resulted in a theoretical cease-fire in many areas of southern and western Sudan.

Negotiations, which center on the place of the south in Sudan, security arrangements, and equal distribution of wealth to all its citizens, give many people hope that a permanent solution to the country's political crises will be found. But, as the respected historian Arnold Toynbee indicates, given the complexity of the conflict, "an agreed settlement can only be reached through forbearance and wisdom on both sides."[18]

Facts About Sudan

GOVERNMENT

Military regime since 1989

President: General Omar Hassan Ahmad al-Bashir (since 1989)

DATE OF INDEPENDENCE

January 1, 1956 (from Egypt and Britain)

NATIONAL HOLIDAYS

Independence Day, January 1 (1956)

PEOPLE

Population: 34,475,690 (1999 estimate)

Capital: Khartoum

Nationality: Sudanese

Languages: Arabic (official), Nubian, Ta Bedawie, Nuer, Dinka, English

Ethnicities: Black, 52 percent (includes Dinka, Nur, Shilluk, and many others); Arab, 39 percent; Beja, 6 percent; foreigners, 2 percent

Religion: Sunni Muslim, 70 percent (in the north); indigenous beliefs, 25 percent; Chrisianity, 5 percent (mostly in the south and Khartoum)

Literacy rate: 46.1 percent

Workforce: Of a total workforce of 11 million, 80 percent work in agriculture; 11 percent in government; 9 percent in industry

Life expectancy: 56.4 years

Infant mortality: 70.94 deaths/1,000 live births

Annual population growth: 2.71 percent

GEOGRAPHY

Area: 966,757 square miles (2,503,890 square kilometers)

Coastline: 629 miles (853 kilometers)

Climate: Tropical in the south; arid desert in the north

Lowest point: Sea level

Highest point: Mt. Kinyeti, 10,457 feet (3,187 meters)

ECONOMY

Currency: Sudanese dinar

Inflation rate (consumer prices): 10 percent (2001 estimate)

Unemployment rate: 18.1 percent (2002 estimate)

Exports: Cotton, sesame, livestock/meat, gum arabic, oil and petroleum products, groundnuts (peanuts), sugar

Imports: Foodstuff, manufactured goods, medicine and chemicals, textiles, refinery and transport equipment, wheat

National debt: $24.9 billion (2000 estimate)

Natural resources: Petroleum; small reserves of iron, copper, chromium, zinc, tungsten, mica, silver, gold

NOTES

INTRODUCTION: TWO NATIONS

1. Francis M. Deng, *Dinka of Sudan.* New York: Holt, Rinehart and Winston, 1972, p. 31.

CHAPTER 1: AN INTRICATE AND VARIED LANDSCAPE

2. Rowlinson Carter, "The Wonder of the Nile," in *The Nile,* eds. Andrew Eames et al. Singapore: APA, 1992, p. 24.

3. Carter, *The Nile,* p. 24.

4. K.M. Barbour, *The Republic of the Sudan: A Regional Geography.* London: University of London Press, 1964, p. 38.

5. Barbour, *The Republic of the Sudan,* p. 44.

CHAPTER 2: THE SUDANESE PEOPLE

6. Emil Ludwig, *The Nile: The Life-Story of a River,* trans. Mary H. Lindsay. New York: Viking Press, 1937, p. 173.

CHAPTER 3: A LAND OF EMPIRES AND KINGDOMS

7. P.L. Shinnie, *Meroe: A Civilization of the Sudan.* London: Thames and Hudson, 1967, p. 161.

8. Quoted in Oliver Albino, *The Sudan: A Southern Viewpoint.* London: Oxford University Press, 1970, p. 18.

CHAPTER 4: CONTEMPORARY SUDAN

9. Interview with Sudanese president Omer Hassan Ahmed al-Bashir, International Reports, 2001. www.international reports.net.

10. Interview with al-Bashir.

11. LexicOrient. "Khartoum: The Village Capital," *Adventures of Sudan.* http://lexicorient.com.

CHAPTER 5: THE CHALLENGES OF EVERYDAY LIFE

12. Robert O. Collins, *Sudan: A Country Study.* ed. Helen Chapin Metz. Washington, DC: Federal Research Division, 1992, p. 127.

13. Sudan 101, "Baggara." www.sudan101.com.

14. Janice Boddy, *Women and Alien Spirits.* Madison: University of Wisconsin Press, 1989, p. 44.

15. Cathy Majtenyi, "Ducking Antonovs an Everyday Reality in South Sudan Classroom," Africanews. www.peacelink.it.

16. Collins, *Sudan*, p. 99.

CHAPTER 6: ARTS AND CULTURE

17. Quoted in editorial, Embassy of the Republic of Sudan, April 2, 2003. www.sudanembassy.org.

18. Quoted in Albino, *The Sudan*, p. V.

CHRONOLOGY

2400 B.C.
The kingdom of Cush develops.

712
Nubians conquer Egypt.

617
Nubians are driven out of Egypt by the Assyrians.

590
Nubia moves its capital to Meroe.

A.D. 500
Nubian kingdoms of Alodia, Alwa, and Maqurra develop.

540
Nubia becomes a Christian kingdom.

642
First wave of Arab migration to Alodia and Maqurra territories.

1300
Second wave of Arab migration—northern Sudan converts to Islam.

1500
Alwa falls to the Funj Kingdom from central Sudan.

1600
Funj Kingdom is at its peak.

1821
Egypt conquers the Funj and the Maqurra territories.

1874
British general George Gordon appointed governor of Sudan.

1876
Egypt gains control of most of present-day Sudan.

1881
Muhammad Ahmad (the Mahdi) leads a revolt against
Egypt.

1882–1885
The Mahdi captures Khartoum; General Gordon is killed
during the attack.

1885
The Mahdi dies of typhoid fever; the Khalifa leads the
Mahdist group.

1896
British and Egyptian forces invade Sudan.

1898–1899
British and Egyptian forces recapture Sudan; the Khalifa is
killed; Anglo Egyptian rule begins.

1953
Sudan is granted self-government by Britain and Egypt.

1955
A transitional government is formed; the political conflict
between north and south begins.

1956
Sudan becomes an independent republic (January 1).

1958
First military coup; General Ibrahim Abboud becomes
president.

1964
Government is forced to step down; rebellion breaks out in
the south.

1969
Second military coup; Colonel Gaafar Nimeiri becomes
president.

1971
Nimeiri is elected president during general elections.

1972

Nimeiri gives autonomous regional government to the
south, ending the north-south conflict.

1983

Nimeiri imposes Islamic law on the whole country; rebellion breaks out in the south in response.

1985

A military coup overthrows Nimeiri's government.

1986

Elections are held; Saliq al-Mahdi becomes president.

1989

Brigadier General Omar Hassan Ahmed al-Bashir
overthrows the al-Mahdi government in an Islamic
fundamentalist–inspired military coup.

1993

The military appoints al-Bashir president.

1996

Al-Bashir elected president; the south boycotts the
elections.

2000

Al-Bashir reelected president.

2002

Peace talks continue.

WORKS CONSULTED

BOOKS

Oliver Albino, *The Sudan: A Southern Viewpoint.* London: Oxford University Press, 1970. Provides the historical, political, economic, and social factors underlying the long political conflict and civil war in Sudan, from the South's perspective.

Georges Balandier and Jacques Maquet, *Dictionary of Black African Civilization.* New York: Leon Amiel, 1974. Provides valuable information on different aspects of African culture and peoples, from arts to games to architecture to religious beliefs.

K.M. Barbour, *The Republic of the Sudan: A Regional Geography.* London: University of London Press, 1964. Provides information on the geography of Sudan and gives a brief overview of the diverse lifestyles of the various peoples.

Janice Boddy, *Women and Alien Spirits.* Madison: University of Wisconsin Press, 1989. Useful analysis on the life of Sudanese women.

Donna Lee Bowen and Evelyn A. Early, eds., *Everyday Life in Muslim Middle East,* Bloomington: Indiana University Press, 2002. Details the experiences of students and teachers in rural villages in the center of Sudan.

Robert Collins, *Sudan: A Country Study.* Helen Chapin Metz, ed., Washington, DC: Federal Research Division, 1992. An overview of the historical, economic, social, and political aspects of Sudan.

C. Brian Cox, ed., *African Writers*, vols. 1 and 2. New York: Charles Scribner's Sons, 1997. Provides good background information on contemporary African writers.

Francis M. Deng, *Dinka of Sudan.* New York: Holt, Rinehart and Winston, 1972. Gives a personal analysis of life among the Dinkas of Sudan.

101

————, *Wars of Vision: Conflict of Identities in the Sudan.* Washington, DC: The Brookings Institution, 1995. Provides an analysis of the history and politics that have contributed to the endemic civil war in Sudan.

Diagram Group, *Encyclopedia of African Peoples.* New York: The Diagram Group, 2000. Gives an impressive overview of the major ethnic groups in Africa—their history, culture, and way of life.

Andrew Eames et al., eds., *The Nile.* Singapore: APA, 1992. Contains interesting essays on different aspects of the Nile River.

P.M. Holt, *A Modern History of Sudan.* New York: Grove Press, 1961. Details the political history of Sudan from the Funj Sultanate to 1958. It is a must-read for anybody interested in the history of modern Sudan.

Emil Ludwig, *The Nile, The Life-Story of a River.* Trans. Mary H. Lindsay. New York: Viking Press, 1937. An old book, but contains some useful personal accounts of travels in Sudan and Egypt.

Keith Lye and the Diagram Group, *Encyclopedia of African Nations and Civilizations.* New York: The Diagram Group, 2002. A good source of information on the various African nations—their political and social histories.

John Middleton, ed., *Peoples of Africa.* New York: Arco, 1979. Helpful information on different African ethnic groups.

Sean Moroney, *Handbooks to the Modern World*, vol. 1. New York: Facts On File, 1989. Brief study of the history, politics, and economy of African countries.

Joyce Moss and Lorraine Valestuk, *World Literature and Its Times*, vol. 2. Detriot: The Gale Group, 2000. Profiles of notable African writers and the historical events that influenced them.

Scott Peterson, *Me Against My Brother.* New York: Routledge, 2000. Gives moving accounts of the human cost of war in Sudan, Somalia, and Rwanda.

George Rodger, *Village of the Nubas.* Hong Kong: Phaidon, 1999. An account of the author's experiences among the Nuba.

John Ryle, *Warriors of the White Nile: The Dinka.* New York: Time-Life Books, 1982. Details the author's experiences among the Dinka of southern Sudan.

P.L. Shinnie, *Meroe: A Civilization of the Sudan.* London: Thames and Husdon, 1967. Detailed information on the history and archaeological findings on the Nubian-Cush city of Meroe and its civilization.

WEBSITES

Embassy of the Republic of Sudan (www.sudanembassy. org). The home site of the embassy of the Republic of Sudan in the United States. The site provides news briefs as well as information on various aspects of Sudanese culture, history, and politics.

International Reports (www.internationalreports.net). A website hosted by the *Washington Post* that gives editorials and reports on current events in Africa.

LexicOrient (http://lexicorient.com). A website designed to provide information on nations of northern Africa, and the Middle East. Articles are brief and written for a general audience.

Sudan 101 (www.sudan101.com). This site, maintained by a Christian organization, contains a variety of factual articles on Sudan and links to other online publications and sites.

USC—University of Southern California, Higher Education Systems Database (www.usc.edu). The site offers an overview of the education system of all countries.

INDEX

Picture Credits

ABOUT THE AUTHOR

Dr. Salome C. Nnoromele is associate professor and coordinator of the graduate program in the department of english and theater at Eastern Kentucky University. She obtained her BA from the University of Utah and both her MA and PhD from the University of Kentucky. A native of Nigeria, Dr. Nnoromele researches, teaches, and writes on various aspects of African literature, culture, and history. Her areas of specialty include nineteenth-century British literature, African and African-American literature, and postcolonial studies, and she is currently the Co-Director of the University of Kentucky's African/African-American Studies program. This is her fourth book for Lucent Books.